From Menifee To Ohio –

The Ginter Family:

An Autobiography by Otto Fleenor Ginter

Copyright

Contents

Dedication to Pop Ginter (1884-1971)

John Cleveland(Cleve) Ginter

Preface

This is a true story, wrote by me, Otto(Ott) Ginter. This is about the John Cleveland and Bessie(Rollins) Ginter family and the twenty years I lived at home, and the almost eighty years I have been associated with the Ginter family. The things about my Grandparents, some of them was told to me by my Parents. The rest is from memory(I lived them). This is about how the Ginter family lived in the mountains of Menifee County, Kentucky, in the pioneer times of the early 1900's, and when we moved from Kentucky to Ohio, and how we lived through the Great Depression. I am not a writer, nor am I a educated man. I was a high school dropout. This story is how I remember it.

Living in the mountains of Eastern Kentucky during the pioneer days of the early 1900s, in Menifee County, Kentucky, there was no electricity. Heat and light was by wood and coal oil. Transportation was by wagon, horseback, or walking. There was no industry. You farmed and raised your food. There was good hunting and fishing, and plenty of berries. To make some money, you dug wild roots, such as ginseng, ginger, may apple, golden seal, and lady slipper. Also, you trapped wild animals for fur. All of these things were taken to Ilinois and sold at the markets. In 1929, during the great depression, we moved to Montgomery County, Ohio.

This story is about how we, as a large family, made it from Kentucky, through the great depression, and into Ohio. All of the things you read here will be covering topics such as the early years in Kentucky, alcohol, automobiles, government, schools, coming to Ohio, and any other things that I thought was important to tell.

Before our family ever saw electricity, automobiles, or factory work in Ohio, we lived deep in the mountains of Menifee County, Kentucky. Life there demanded hard work, courage, and neighbors who depended on one another to survive. What follows is the story of those mountain years—of Beaver Creek, Leatherwood Branch, and the Ginter family who carved a life out of the hills before the Great Depression changed everything.

There will never be another generation that goes through as hard of times as it was way back then.   -Ott Ginter

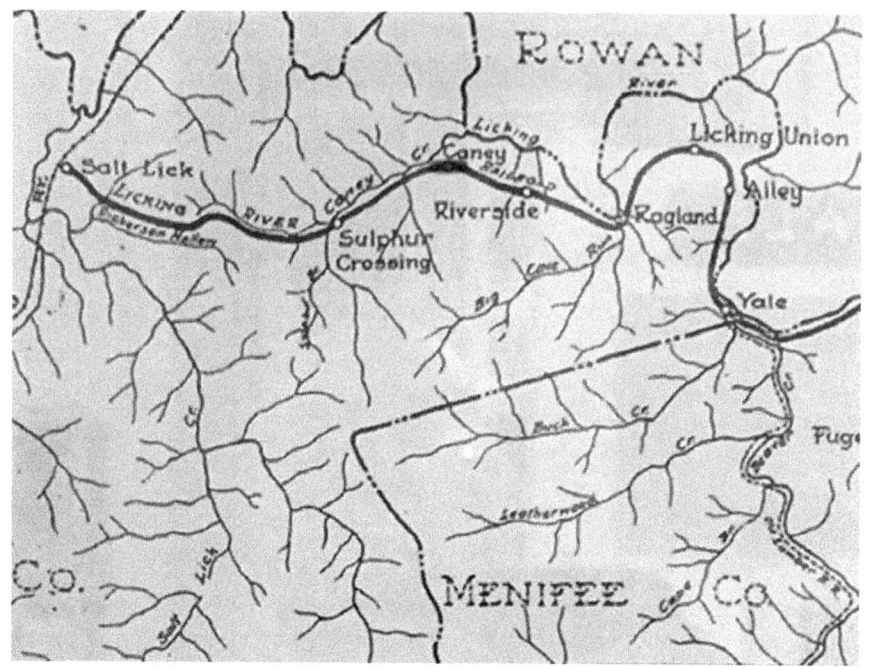

Licking River, Beaver Creek, and Leatherwood Branch - @1912

Chapter I (1915-1929)

Life In Menifee County, Kentucky

Beaver Valley and Beaver Creek

Beaver Valley and Beaver Creek was in the mountains of Menifee County Kentucky. Beaver Valley started at Frenchburg, Kentucky to Salt Lick, Kentucky, which is a total of about thirty miles. Beaver Creek run from Frenchburg, Kentucky about twenty miles down to the Licking River. Beaver Valley was about one and a half to two miles wide, with Beaver Creek running down close to the foot of the mountains. On each side of Beaver Valley was thousands and thousands of virgin timber.

This was in the middle and latter parts of the 1800's. A railroad company run a spur railroad line up Beaver and opened up the territory to logging. Log camps and sawmills were all over the territory, and work was plentiful. This lasted quite a few years, then timber was getting scarce, and the logging camps and sawmills started laying off workers. The railroad took out it's spur line. Some of the workers went elsewhere, and some purchased land up and down Beaver Valley.

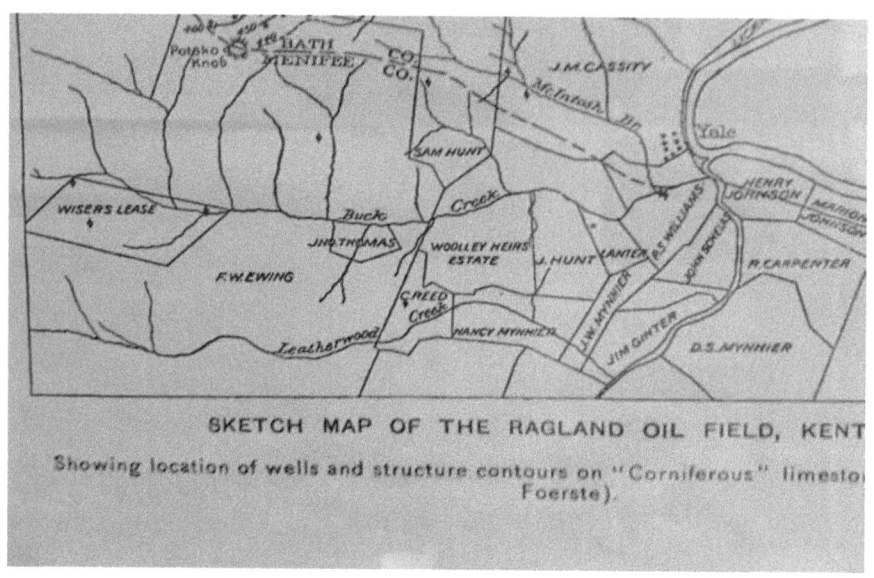

James Monroe Ginter Property - @1912

Grandpa James Monroe Ginter

1848-1918

The Old Ginter Homeplace and the Ginter Cemetery

Grandpa James Monroe Ginter took his family and roamed the West. He settled in Oklahoma for awhile, then came back home. He settled down on Beaver Creek, just below Leatherwood. He purchased land and settled there. This was the Old Ginter Homeplace. It was in Menifee County, Kentucky. Grandpa made his living farming, and he raised a very large family there at the old home place. Grandpa was very active in community affairs, and was a leader in the community.

Grandpa and Grandma had a son that died right after childbirth. Grandpa has a piece of land on top of Leatherwood Hill that was pretty flat. Grandpa buried his son up there and donated a large section to the community for a cemetery. The community named it the Ginter Cemetary. It is still being used to this day. Grandpa lived the rest of his life on the old home place and both Grandpa and Grandma Ginter are buried there.

James Monroe Ginter (1848-1918)

Grandpa Wade Hampton(Hamp) Rollins

1865-1941

The Rollins Family at Leatherwood Branch

In the latter part of the 1800's, Grandpa Rollins lived in Greenup,

Kentucky. He was in the sawmill business, mostly sawing stave
bolts for barrel manufacturing companies. Timber was getting
scarce, so Grandpa purchased 600 acres of land at the mouth of
Leatherwood Branch, with his land running back into the
mountains. Grandpa built a two story house at the mouth of
Leatherwood Branch, and a General Store. He moved his sawmill
business to the mouth of Leatherwood. Down past Grandpa's
house, he donated some ground and built a school house. It was
called the Leatherwood School House. Grandpa Rollins was
known as a just and fair employer. Grandpa and Grandma Rollins
lived out their lives at the mouth of Leatherwood Branch, and are
buried in the Ginter Cemetary.

Gpa Wade Hampton Rollins and Gma Sarah Prudence (Miller)
Rollins

Cleve and Bessie Ginter get some land and build a house

John Cleveland Ginter was my Father. Cleve Ginter met Bessie
Rollins at a country dance, where Cleve was playing the banjo with
a band. They courted for awhile, and in the early part of 1900, they
got married. Cleve bought one hundred and seventeen acres of land
from his Father-In-Law, Hamp Rollins, up above Leatherwood, at
Haystack Holler. There were about fifteen acres of flat bottom and,
suitable for tending(farming). The rest was in mountains. The top

of the mountain was what was called Hillside Flat. This meant that the tops could be cleared off of trees and bushes, and made what we called new ground. It could be used to raise crops. Haystack Holler run down between two mountains and emptied into Beaver Valley.

At the mouth of Haystack Holler is where Cleve and Bessie built their home. It was a traditional mountain home. It was built with heavy planks with strips over the cracks, never was painted on the outside. The inside was insulated with heavy felt paper that was nailed to the walls. The house was built ina "L" shape. It had four rooms and a porch on the "L" side and one on the branch side. The roof had hand made wood shingles that Cleve made. Cleve built a chimney on one end of the house for heating. He made most of the furniture, like the kitchen table, benches for the kitchen table, and chairs with split wood bottoms. Cleve would make the wood splits and Bessie would weave them. To make the splits, he would go back into the woods to find white oak limbs the size he wanted. Then he would split off the bark. Then he would start making the splits to size. He would take pieces of glass and smooth them down. They were about 1/16" thick and about 1/8" wide. Of course you could make different sizes. They also weaved all kinds of baskets out of these splits.

Bessie would order all colors of dye to make colored baskets. she made the bed ticks(mattresses). The ticks would be stuffed with corn shucks. The pillows would be stuffed with feathers. Then you would have a feather bed. Bessie made all of the bed quilts. She would order cloth remnants from a mail order company and sew them together and use other material for the bottoms, and if possible, put some kind of cotton or yarn in between and then they are quilted together(sewed together with stitch rows about 1 ½" apart).

Cleve also needed farming animals and farming equipment. He bought a team of horses for plowing, hauling, and to ride for transportation. He needed a turn plow, a harrow and drag, a double shovel plow, and a single shovel plow. He needed a wagon and a sled. The sled to haul where you couldn't with a wagon. He needed harnesses for the horses, a saddle, a milk cow for milk, a few chickens to lay eggs. There was a good cold spring up at the head of the holler. Drinking water was carried from here. Cleve and Bessie had built their home and bought the things they needed to make a living, so they were ready to start housekeeping and to start a family.

1916-Pop, Mom, Walter, Me, Raymond

Mom & Pop Begin Their Family

In about a year their first child was born, a boy. They named him Raymond. The next child was a boy and his name was Walter. Then the next child was a very little boy, and his name was Otto(Me). I only weighed a little over two pounds. Mom said I weighed two and one half pounds. I was so small she put me in a wool sock and placed it in a shoe box and put me behind the wood heatin' stove.

The nights were starting to get cold. Pop went and bought the stove. We heated with a fireplace until I was born. The stove was my incubator. I was born by a mid-wife who lived in the area. She rode side-saddle to my folks place. There were no doctors or hospitals. The next was a boy. His name was Austin. Low and behold, the next was a girl and her name was Marie. The next was another boy and his name was Adrian. The last was a girl, named Virginia. A mid-wife took care of the births.

Childhood in the Mountains (1920 and After)

School Days

I was born in 1915, and it was about 1920 when I started to remember life with the Ginter's. You see, this was pioneer times in the mountains, as there were no electric. All lighting was done by coal oil lamps and lanterns. No industry, you had to raise what you eat and make the most of the things you wore.

After the lumber business shut down, there were no jobs. In the early days, there were no cars. Your transportation was riding a horse, by wagon, or walking. Almost every household had a rifle and shotgun for hunting. Also, a good double bit ax and cross-cut saw to cut wood for heating and cooking. That way, with the water close, that it would not get hot enough to catch fire. Above our house, Beaver Creek had a

bend in it, and at the bend there was a small field. The men in the community would hue out railroad ties by hand and bring them to this place and fasten them together on land, and wait for the fall rains, when Beaver Creek raised above flood stage, then float the rafts down Beaver to the Licking River, then up the Licking River to a town along the river and sell them. This was a hard way to get a little money. If ten men had eleven cross ties apiece, ties in those days, 7" X 9" was selling for $.60 each. Ten men with 11 ties each would be ninety-nine feet long, and each man would get $6.60.

I was old enough to go to school by then, so I started at the Leatherwood School. I can remember that I got into a fight the first day. We had a man teacher and he let us fight, but he would stand by with a switch, and if one of the fighters would do something unfair, he would wharp them with the switch. The school house only had one room with three rows of seats. The seats were wide enough for two students. The Two outside row run up about 2/3 the length of the room, the middle row about half way because of the heating stove. The blackboard was on the back wall. The teacher's desk was next to the blackboard.

In front of the teacher's desk was a long bench. This is where all classes were held. First grade through Eighth. The first thing in the morning when school was taken up, the first grade was called up for their first subject, then through the eighth grade, and then it would start all over again with the next subject until all grades had their lessons.

The school only had one privey that was used by both boys and girls. They had a code for using the privey during school hours. A book in or by the door if the privey was in use, no book, all clear.

The teacher would take the school on hikes to learn about the wildlife. In the mountains, there was a dug water well. It had the sides closed off, and a rope and a pulley to draw up water in a bucket. All of the school children were required to have their own metal telescoping drinking cup. All the children had to walk to school. Most of them wore homemade clothes, and in the summer, they went barefoot. In those days the school year was seven months.

There were somewhat under thirty children that went to Leatherwood School. Up Beaver was the Kring children. Down farther were the Charles, on down were the Ginter children. Next was up Leatherwood. The first was the Mynhier children, next was the Gillespie children, and on up was the Profitt children. Back Down Beaver was the Robinson children, and across Beaver was the Montgomery children. On down Beaver there was another Robinson family. That is the children that went to school when I did.

I enjoyed going to Leatherwood School. I think in them old mountain schools we learned more through the eighth grade than high school pupils learn today. You could get a grade school education at Leatherwood School. If you wanted to go to high school, you could go to Frenchburg. If you wanted to go to college, you had to go to Moorehead.

The next year, I got my first labor contract. It was building a fire early in the morning in the wintertime in the schoolhouse, for a nickel a morning, or twenty-five cents a week. I think that some politics was in me getting the job, for Pop was the school trustee, and he hired the teachers.

I was still getting in fights, and would win some, lose some, and some were a draw. I got disciplined a few times. Seems as tho the teachers attitude had changed since we had women teachers.

Leatherwood School Me, Randolph 1964

Lessons From Pop: Work, Tools, and Survival Skills

While growing up, Pop started teaching us the things we needed to know like how to survive in times, like in the mountain pioneer days. Of course, I was nosey, I wanted to know how you did this, and why you did it. Pop was a good teacher. He always had time to show and explain things.

When Pop first took me along with Raymond and Walter, on top of the mountain to hoe corn, I would be going along chopping weeds like snakes, and Pop would be going along as smooth and easy as

21

like it was nothing. I would say to Pop, "I know what the problem is. You have got a better and sharper hoe than mine." Pop would say, "Here, I'll swap with you." We would swap hoes, and there would be Pop going along using my hoe as easy as pie, and me going along making a hard job of cutting the weeds.

Finally, Pop said, "Here, I'll show you how to use a hoe. You don't chop with a hoe, you place it above the weeds and put pressure on the handle, and pull toward you."

Next, Pop taught us how to shoe a horse. You take a special knife and trim off the surplus hoof. Then you take a rasp and smooth it up even, and start fitting the shoe. If the shoe doesn't fit, then rasp off some more till it fits. When nailing on the shoes with horseshoe nails, you have to be careful. The safe way is to bend the nail slightly on the end, so the nail comes out the side of the hoof, and not up into the quick. Then you cut the nails, leaving them about ¼" long, so they will hold when clinched, or bent over.

Next lesson was why a horse had to have a set of harnesses. To pull with a set of harnesses was a padded collar that fit around the horses neck, with leather outside. This leather part was grooved for the horses hames to fit in. A leather strap on each side of the horse that runs back to almost the length of the horse. A length of chain was fastened onto this leather strap This was to pull with. A wide leather strap across the horses back his hips, one from the pulling chain around under the tail, and a belly band that fastened to each of the pulling chains.

Pop taught us boys a great many things, like how to butcher and dress out a hog, and to use common sense while doing anything. When we would be working in the fields, there would be me, Pop, Raymond, Walter, and sometimes Austin. Sometimes before dinner time, Pop would say to me, "Go to the house and get some stove wood for your Ma to get dinner." On other days, he would say, "You stay at home and help your Ma do the washing.", or, "Quit early and go to the store for your Ma." Seems as though when Mom needed help, I was the one that was given the job of helping her. I was afraid to complain. If I did, Pop just might give the job to one of the other boys, and I didn't want that because I just loved helping Mom. In the summertime, after we quit for the day, us boys would head for Beaver and go swimming. After that we would do our chores, like milking cows, feeding the horses and hogs. Sometimes we would have to go back on the mountain to herd the cows in. After supper, we would head to Beaver again to fish. Beaver Creek was only about five hundred yards from the house pike, sunfish, redeyes, and a lot of bullfrogs. Some evenings, two of the boys would take the boat up Beaver to the abandoned Bolden place, and the other two would go across the mountain and gather pinenots for the boat's fire basket. This was the light to see to gig. Then we would go back down Beaver about 9P.M. and gig for frogs and fish. Light from these pinenots would penetrate the water deeper than any other kind of lighting. Once in awhile, Pop would go with us on these gigging trips.

One day Pop said, "Come along boys, we are going to make some roofing shingles to patch the roof on the house." First, he said we will saw a length of the log laying in the wood yard. Next, Pop went in the tool shed and brought out what he called a froe. First, you would take the handle of the froe in your left hand and then you wood take the wood mallet in your righthand and hit the flat part of the froe blade to start the froe blade into the wood. Then you would pull toward you on the froe handle. This would cause it to split. Next, you would want to split the round sides from the block making it square. When the block is square, if wide enough, split into two pieces. This way you will have more wood to make the shingles. Now you can start splitting the shingles. That is how it was done in the old days.

Now Pop said we will go back on the mountain with the team and snake some of those logs over to the log dump. We will need to take a pair of grabs, a pair of spreaders, two single trees, and a can't hook. We had been cutting timber(logs) for about a year and let them lay back on the mountain. Now it was time to get them to a place up the holler behind the house. When pulling these logs with horses, you used the following equipment. A set of grabs with the sharp ends drove in each side of the log. Then a set of spreaders with single trees hooked to the grabs. There was a swivel between the grabs and spreader. This swivel was a safety to keep the horses. If the log would roll, this swivel kept the horses from getting tangles up in the harness.

The can't hook was to turn the log over to start it rolling down to the dump. The dump was up the holler behind the house. These logs landed in and piled up in the holler at the foot of the mountain.

Pop borrowed Grandpa Rollins saw mill and set it up in the holler close to the log dump and begain sawing lumber, railroad ties, and all kinds of other lumber. We had to hire one man, and that was Uncle Ernest Rollins, who was an experienced sawyer. Pop fired the boiler, Raymond snaked the logs in to the mill, me and Walter offbearded. We took the sawed lumber and etc. from the conveyer to the lumber yard, which was a flat place across the branch. The sawdust from the mill, we saved part of it and let the branch carry the rest away. On the weekends, we would stack the lumber to let it kill dry. Then we started to haul it to market. When this project was done, Pop said, "Boys, we need more ground to tend. I think that we will clear off a new ground on that mountain on the other side of the house." So we cut down the big trees and blasted out the stumps, cleared off all the brush, and we had a new ground field ready to plow and plant.

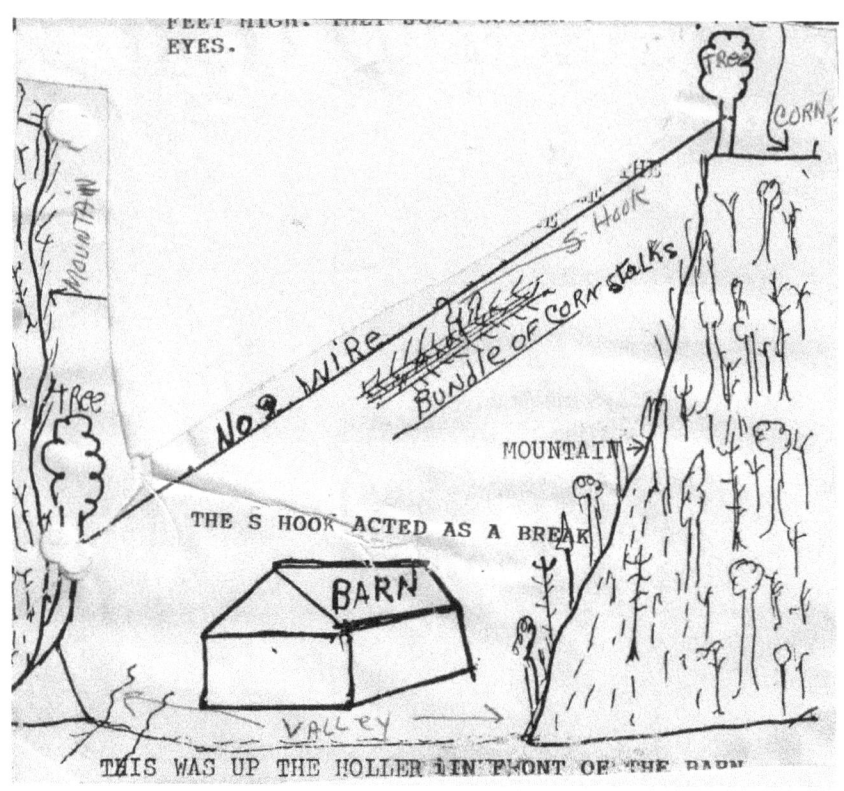

Corn Zip Line

Pop said, "I have an idea that will save us a lot of work and we are not going to have to go around and up the mountain on the Leatherwood side to bring the corn off the mountain on a sled. I'm going to Frenchburg when we get the new ground cleared. I have a idea when I get back, we will see if it works." When the ground was cleared, Pop went to Frenchburg and come back with a roll of #9 smooth wire. We stretched the wire from a tree on top at the cornfield and the other end to a tree at the foot of the barn. The corn was tied in a bundle and with a S wire hooked on the wire.

This brought the corn down in the barnyard. In the early twenties, some Model T Fords started to appear. Grandpa Rollins purchased one. Also, Sherman Kring and Farmer Sorrell, and a fellow working for the Eureka Oil Company by the name of Red Black had one.

Hunting, Fishing, and Mountain Adventures

Along Beaver and back in the mountains there were fur bearing animals such as possum, fox, coons, wild cats, squirell, rabbits, mink, muskrats. We had trap lines set and we did a lot of night hunting. I can remember one time Raymond, me, and Walter started to go hunting. We were going up the mountain by the house and we came to a large flat rock and set down to rest. The country road run along close to the house. A old model T was coming up the road and it stopped and a man hollered, "Put that light up there out or I will shoot it out." Well, that didn't scare us. We set the lantern on the rock and got behind some big tree's and hollered back, "You got it to do." Then he started shooting and those bullets were going W—H—I—N—G out through the treetops. We heard Pop holler and say, "Cut that shooting out and I mean now." Well the man quit and next day Pop said it was Red Black and he was drunk. We went on hunting and pretty soon the dog treed a possum. Raymond said, "Stand back and I'll shoot him." Walter said, "No, you will ruin his fur. I'll climb up and catch him." Walter climbed up that tree and we heard him holler ouch. Pretty soon that ole possum come down that tree leading ole Walter by the finger and wouldn't let loose. We finally got Walter loose from that ole possum. And we went on hunting. Pretty soon the dogs treed a skunk back in a cave. Raymond said to me, "Hold up the light so I can see to shoot it." So I holds up the lantern and B-I-N-G-O that old skunk squirted me just above the hair line. I said, "Boys, that's it, lets go home." When we got to the house I was going to open the door. It opened and Mom said, "Which one has been waltzing with a skunk?" Well that was me and I had to pull off my clothes and leave them on the outside and go out to the branch and try to wash the smell off.

Well, the next Sunday Pop and Mom went to visit the neighbors. Us boys was getting tired of carrying drinking water from the head of the holler, so we started digging a well by the back porch. When Pop and Mom came home we were pretty far down. Pop helped us finish digging it and when we hit water we carries rocks and he walled it up. Then we built a wooden frame around the top and put a bar across and fastened a pully and rope and bucket to draw up water.

It was the weekend when we got the job done, so Sunday us boys decided to go back in the mountains exploring. So we started down the road to go upon the mountain and here comes our sister Marie following us. We had been outrunning her, but she was getting big enough that we couldn't outrun her anymore. So we would take the ball of our foot and make a snake track across the dusty road and that was as far as Marie would go. We would go on back in the mountains where nobody else went looking for caves and any funny looking rocks. Of course we were always looking for ginseng. We would come back by the place below the limestone cliff, on top of the mountain where Pop was prospecting for gold. Times when we had nothing to do, Pop would take us up there and help where he was digging a shaft. We never did find any gold.

Daily Life: Farming, Preserving Food, and Mountain Survival

Like I said, it was in the pioneer days in Menifee County, Kentucky. In those days there were no industries, no jobs to be had after the lumber mills shut down. You had to raise about everything you needed to live, to raise it and preserve it to make the winter. There was plenty of blackberrys and raspberrys on the mountainsides, and huckleberrys on top of the cliffs on top of the mountains. You canned blackberrys, raspberrys, made black and raspberry jam and jelly, canned huckleberrys. You would bury potatoes in the ground. You would dig out a shallow place in the ground and place straw in it. Then pile the potatoes on this straw and put straw on top of the potatoes, and then cover the potatoes over with dirt. Enough dirt that the potatoes would be below the freezing mark.In the winter time when you wanted some potatoes you would dig a small hole in the mound big enough to get your hand in to get some potatoes. You would put some straw in the graveling hole and cover with dirt. You would bury apples the same way. Cabbage you did a little different. You placed the heads facing each other, follow the same process as for potatoes and apples. You would can green beans, cucumber pickles, peaches. About everybody had apple and peach tree's. You canned sweet corn. If you had a large family you made a barrel of sour kraut, raised sage and black pepper, raised peanuts, raised cane and made sorguhm mollases, raised broom corn and took it to the factory in Salt Lick and they would make you brooms and take a toll for making them. You would raise pumpkins and shell beans in the cornfields along with the corn. Mom canned all these things. Of course, with the help of the whole family. We would take ground hogs skin and bury them in wood aches and this would tan them and we would make shoe strings and other strings from the hides.

To have ice for the summertime we would build a ice house with about a two foot liner in it. We would fill this liner up with saw dust. In the winter time, when Beaver was froze over, cut blocks of ice and fill the ice house.

You had to do a lot of planning and have the know-how to survive in those pioneer days. We trapped and hunted, and tanned the hides such as possum, coons, muskrats and mink. We dug all kinds of herbs, such as ginseng, yellow root(golden seal), lady slipper. This had a bloom on top in shape of a ladies slipper. We dug ginger and mayapple, red root. All these growed on the mountains. Golden seal was selling for three dollars a pound dried. Ginseng was selling for one dollar an ounce, lady slipper about two dollars and ginger from six cent to ten cents a pound. All these herbs were dried and all furs tanned. They were shipped to Chicago mail order company buying herbs and furs. The money we got for this went toward paying the taxes on the place and to buy something you couldn't raise. You would raise hogs to butcher for meat and lard, sausage and some of the intrails were used to make soap. The maple trees were tapped in the early spring to make maple syrup. Mom raised chickens to have eggs for the family. Us boys caught fish out of Beaver as there were plenty of all kinds.

There were some incidents that happened like one time Raymond was plowing corn in the field below the garden and Mom was taking him a drink, when out at the end of the row she saw a large rattlesnake. She thought she would have a little fun with Raymond. She goes up to the garden and gets a hoe. When Raymond comes out to the end she touched the snake with the hoe to get it to rattle and scare Raymond. She touched it with the hoe and nothing happened so she touched him again putting more pressure on the hoe. Still no movement. She called Raymond and they examined the snake and found out it was dead. It had tried to crawl under a rock and the rock had come down on his head, killing it.

One other time when Raymond, Walter, and me were going ginseng hunting we were going up the mountain at the head of the holler, when we stopped to rest and Walter had stopped with right foot on a log. He was holding hid ginseng digger in his hand and he looked down and lo and behold a ole snake had slipped up and layed his head by Walter's foot. Walter just went P-I-N-G with that ginseng digger and got that ole snake right through the head. Walter jumped over the hill one way and the snake went a flopping the other way.

About that time someone hollered down at the foot of the mountain. It was Austin. He was following us so we took him along with us. We were going along by a cliff and there was a cave back in it and an ole buzzard had her nest in back of it. We had always heard if you caught a buzzard it would vomit on you. Well, we talked Austin in going back in the cave and getting her. Well, he did, and that old story about them vomiting was just a story. That ole buzzard was real friendly and didn't do a thing We went on looking for ginseng. Pretty soon the dogs had something treed over on the other mountain. Our dogs always went with us where ever we went. We went over to see what they were barking at and they had a big snake bayed on the ground. He was too big for them to shake to death. We killed the snake. None of us boys never got snake bitten. I think our dogs got credit for that. They were death on finding and killing snakes and most the time we went bare footed.

Like the incident that happened to me. One time Mom told me to go down to Yale and get the mail. There was no saddle available so I thought I would stop at Grandpa Rollins and borrow his. I found a pair of spurs in the barn, so I buckled them on. Going down to

Grandpa's I was riding bare back and ole Charley got to galloping and I couldn't keep the spurs from gouging him in the flanks. By the time we got to Grandpa's I couldn't get him stopped for he was running away with me. About a mile below Grandpa's I got smart and held my feet out so the spurs wouldn't gouge him anymore. Then I got him stopped. So don't ride a horse with spurs on without a saddle.

Another little incident that happened to Raymond. There was a foot log across Leatherwood and Raymond kept running ahead of Mom and crossing the foot log. Mom kept telling him he was going to fall off and drown. One day he fell off. He jumped out of the water and said, "Am I drowned?

Long Lost Uncle Albert

One day Grandpa Rollins had a long lost brother show up. He was a bachelor and had been roaming the West. He had held about every job there was in the West. We found out that ole man Uncle Albert Rollins, that was his name, was a good carpenter for he went around through the community making the women folks a kitchen cabinet. His charge was ten dollars and they furnish the lumber. The cabinet would have drawers and shelves, also a corn and flour bin. He was a super carpenter and the women of the community kept him busy. I think that he built a cabinet for every household along Beaver. Uncle Albert was more or less a loner. He decided to build a cabin and stay. He bought a piece of land on top of a cliff back from Sooky Branch. The only way up was a path from the other side. I guess he decided to be a hermit. He had a house raising to build the cabin. A bunch of men of the community showed up. They had to take the lumber up with a rope and pulley, but he had a nice cabin setting on a rock on top of a mountain.

One time we had a cow pasture rented up on the Bouldin Place and we put some of our milk cows up there on pasture and we had to go up there twice a day and milk them. That was me and Austin's job to ride horses up there and milk the cows. I rode ole Charley and Austin rode ole Maude. We milked and put the milk in buckets with fastened lids, so the milk wouldn't spill. One day coming back just below the lane that went up to Sherman Krings, ole Maude stepped in a hole in the road and fell down with Austin and ole Austin went scooting along the road holding that milk bucket up. You know he didn't spill a drop of that milk.

One time Pop went hunting with us boys. He said, "I'll show you boys how to really hunt." We were going out through the woods and a squirrel was setting out on a limb. Pop pulled down on him and about that time another squirrel jumped out by the other one. Pop was already pulling the trigger, so he got two squirrels with one shot. So he said, "Boys, there you are." And went back to the house.

Community Life, School, and Social Gatherings

There were social affaires going on in the community, like prayer meetin on Wednesday and church and Sunday school on Sunday. All events were held in the Leatherwood school house. Everybody went to church together. It didn't make any difference what your belief was, you all went to the same church. There was one self ordained preacher. Of course, other preachers would come in from other parts of the county and hold revivals.

The school spelling bee was held at the school house. Spelling was one of my worst subjects and I would be out about the second round.

Another popular event was a fund raising pie supper. The single girls would bake pies and wrap them up in fancy wrappings. They would be auctioned off to the highest bidder. The boys tried to pick the one their girlfriend had brought. Or some of the boys would try to buy some girl's pie in which that girl had a steady and jealous boyfriend. You see, what ever girls pie you bought, you got to eat the pie with her and walk her home. There were some fist fights but a good fundraiser. There were other goings on such as a corn blading. You would put out the word to invite your neighbors to a corn blading party. After dark when the moon was shining, you pulled blades off of the corn stalk from the ear down. In those days there were generally two stalks to a hill and you placed the blades between the stalks for tieing in bundles later. The idea of pulling the blades in moonlight was at that time was a light dew would make them in-case and this would make them easily handled to tie in bundles later.

Another social affair was a bean hulling. Your neighbors would be invited. The idea was to sit around and hull soup beans and drink coffee and catch up on all the gossip. The men sometimes would have something just a little bit stronger than coffee. Another doings was, sometimes on Sunday, the men would go saneing for fish on Beaver, using a sixty foot sane. How they divided them was split them in as many men as there was. One man would turn his back and another one would point to a pile of fish. The man with his back turned would call one of the mens name, until all the piles were gone.

Beaver Valley Incidents and Local Folklore

A few more going on's while we lived along Beaver. Pop decided that he needed a little cash, so he got together with Ernest Rollin, Mom's brother, and they decided to go over to Indinia and work in the onion fields close to Huntertown.

They took Raymond and Walter with them. They borrowed Grandpa Rollins Model T Ford to go up there. They got a job making $18.00 a week. When they come back they said they had thirty-five flat tires on the trip. This left me and Austin to run the farm. When they got back I was anxious to get Walter to one side to see what kind of tobacco he had brought me. It was Velvet. Me and Austin had got Uncle Farm Wells and his sorghum molasses outfit and were making molasses when they got home. Pop said Austin and me had done a good job. Mind now this is in the late twenties. It didn't take the boys long to get back into middle of things like going hunting, fishing, and swimming.

They had a place in Frenchburg that they called the Fras Box. It was something like the Goodwill, you could buy second hand clothes. I can remember me and Pop walking to Frenchburg which was close to fifteen miles. It was a long way to make the trip. Pop bought me a overcoat for $0.25. It was a little large but I was proud of it.

This was getting along toward the late Twenties. Our neighbor up the road had bought a model T Ford car, Farmer Sorrell up on Beaver had bought one, Omar Gillespie up on Leatherwood had bought a Buick touring car, Faris Gillespie had a car that was called a Star car, and of course Grandpa Rollin had a model T Ford. Our closest neighbor Sherman Kring had the only radio in the community and during the week he would jack up his Model T and charge the radio battery, so it would be up for Saturday nite. The neighbors would gather in and listen to the Grand Ole Opry, and the younger ones would square dance. Joe Charles, a neighbor from across Beaver, would come and call the sets. This was mostly every week's get together. These get together's got to be so popular that on Saturday night Sherman would have a full house.

In the winter time Raymond, Walter, and me made it a sport to see who, early in the morning could get up first and build afire in the fireplace, or if there were live coals build the fire up. The family was real close in those days. Mom used to read to the family at least once a week. She would read books like "The Sinking of the Titanic". One book I can remember was the "Little Red Train", or any other book she could get. Next week she would red more from these books. The reading was done by coal oil lamp light. Friday night was a special time.

This nite the entire family would gather around and shell corn to take to the grist mill Saturday to get the weeks corn meal ground. The grist mill was way down in Yale. One of us would ride down there to get this done. We had a special lined sack to carry the cornmeal. The charge to grist mill owner would take a toll of the corn. Mill day was

also the time that the men folks would trade at the Yale store, and sat around and whittle while waiting for there corn to get ground, and to catch up on current affairs.

Scranton Camp Meetings

Up Beaver about six miles was a little town called Scranton. They had a tabernacle and out buildings. This had been built by the community to have a place to hold revivals. They named it the "Camp Meeting Grounds". It got to be an anual event as revivals

38

were held. They lasted for a week and some well known preachers come to the camp preach. It got so popular that people from other states started coming to the camp meetings. There was a large building that was used for a kitchen and there were cabins for those that come from other states and wanted to stay the entire week. The tabernacle was a open air tabernacle, so meetings could only be held in the summertime. I can remember the whole family going up to the camp meeting in a wagon. Sometimes Mom would go up and help cook.

Sometime later the community started a community re-union. Re-unions are still being held today as an annual event. A lot of the people that had never lived in Menifee County comes back to the re-union.

Old Scranton General Store and Post Office 40373

The Traditions of the Mountains

The mountains on each side of the house was rugged and tall. The one on the right of the house, we had tending fields. On top, we also had a peach orchard up there and Grandpa Rollins had fields and a peach orchard joining our land. The mountain on the left was also rough and tall. We had a foot path up both mountains. I can remember one time I was out in the front yard, and looked up the mountain, and a man was coming down the foot path leading a horse. I wondered how in the world he got that horse up on that mountain. He had went up on the end of the mountain.

His name was Ballard, and he stayed all nite with us. It was the custom in the mountains if it got late you stopped and stayed with the nearest family, and you would be welcomed. Your door was not closed to your neighbor or stranger. People would come to your house and holler and then just walk in. And if a loved one died, the neighborhood would hold a wake. When anyone died, it didn't make any difference who. The men of the neighborhood if it was a male and women if it was a female, would prepare the corpse for burial. Someone would donate lumber and the good carpenters of the neighborhood would make a coffin and vault. Some others would dig the grave.

This would be up at the Ginter Cemetary. Some people, neighbors, and family would set with the corpse from the time they died until the funeral. The funeral didn't cost the family anything. All services were donated. Back in those days, the body didn't have to be embalmed, nor a cement vault. Everything was of wood, mostly poplar or Len. This was soft and easy to work with and made beautiful caskets. Did not have to have a death certificate. Everything, you and the neighbors had it to do.

Frenchburg was a nice little mountain town and was the county seat of Menifee County. So we will start and take a trip down Beaver in Menifee County to Yale in Bath County. The road runs from Frenchburg to Salt Lick, but Beaver emptied into the Licking River about twenty miles down. Out from Frenchburg was a road that run out on Dry Ridge. They were quite a few familys lived out on the Ridge. They had a store and had enough children for a school. So Dry Ridge had a school house and had a school district.

Violence and Law in the Mountains

The Ballard Brothers and Revenuers

In these mountains, every once in awhile some violence would occur. It was mostly from every day good ole mountain boys. Mostly with people who lost their temper, or provoked by somebody or something. Like the shoot out at the Dry Ridge school house. They were having an election to elect a school Trustee. When the poles closed the candidate's were tied up and a little ole lady come in and wanted to vote, tho the pole were

41

closed. One side wanted to let her vote to break the tie. The other side didn't. So an argument started and tempers flared and finally got out of hand. Someone pulled a gun and started shooting. Of course this brought more guns into play. When it was all over, two people dead and some wounded.

Like the other incident that happened on Beaver. When a Angram boy shot a Spencer boy. The week before they had got into a rastling match on mill day. The next time it was a fist fight. And later they met in the road and passed one another. Both turned and the Angram boy shot the Spencer boy. The Angram boy pleaded self-defense. He claimed that the Spencer boy put his hand into his pocket and he thought he was going for a gun. He was charged with murder and they had a jury trial. The jury found him guilty on a lesser charge. He was sentenced to three years in the pen in Frankfort. He served one year and was parolled. It was said that his father bought him out, as his father was a leading citizen in the community and was known to have a large bankroll.

On down Beaver was Indian Creek. There were quite a few familys lived upon Indian Creek. There were an incident that happened up on Indian Creek. Three Ballard Brothers had them a moonshine still up at the head of Indian Creek and was making whiskey. Someone turned them in to the Internal Revenue.

Revenue officers came to Frenchburg to the sheriffs office, Ben Wells was the sheriff, and wanted Ben to go up Indian Creek with them to apprehend them. The sheriff refused to go with them. Evidently, they was afraid to go up there alone, so they went to the Ballard home and got two young brothers of the Ballard boys and put them in front of them when the officers went up to the cabin. It was said that Bob Ballard was so angered when he saw his little brothers in front of the Revenue men that he shoved a pistol over his and started shooting at the cabin with high power rifles. They killed Bob, but there was one of the other brothers in the cabin when the shooting started. He climbed up through the cabin's chimney and landed on the hillside and started running, with the Revenue men shooting at him. They wounded him in the heel. He went down Indian Creek and met the Sheriff and a posse coming up to see what had happened, so he surrendered to the sheriff. The posse went on up and met the Revenue coming back down. The Revenue men wanted the sheriff to turn the Ballard over to them. The sheriff refused, the posse and the Revenue men backed off facing each other. Looked like it was going to be a shoot out between the sheriffs posse and Revenue men.

Then the Revenue men saw they couldn't bluff the sheriff, so they backed off. The residents of Menifee County was so outraged at the method the Revenue men used that they told them never again to come into Menifee County. The Internal Revenue Dept. charged the Ballard man with murder, but he swore that he had done no shooting at all. His brother had done all the shooting. And the

Internal Revenue couldn't prove otherwise, so the murder case was thrown out of court.

Menifee County Sheriff Peter Lafayette (Fay) Little

(killed in the line of duty 1934) - with deputies and Federal agents. Little is 3rd left.

Families and Towns Along Beaver and Surrounding Hollers

On down Beaver lived the Spencers, the Bensons, the Sorrells, and some more familys Then we come to Scranton. Scranton had a Post Office, a general store, also the wide known camp meeting grounds where a revival was held for a week once a year. Claude Manns was the post master and owner of the general store. His family was the only residents of Scranton. On down the road along Beaver was Brushy Branch. No one lived here yet. On down Coal Cave were a few familys lived, including Will Whitt and the Tacketts. On down with his house close to the road on one side, and close to Beaver on the other side, lived Green Patrick and family. They could set on their back porch and fish in Beaver.

Next was the Boultin place. Aunt Monnie and Uncle Clay Whitt had it rented and lived there. By the Bouldin place was a long stretch of Beaver that was called Bouldin straight. It was long and deep and was very good fishing. At the end of Bouldin straight was a ripple that run into a whirlpool. The saying was that nobody could find out how deep it was. The saying was some men disappeared exploring it. The next place from the Bouldin place was Murder Branch. John T. Williams lived at the mouth of Murder Branch and one family lived up the branch. Up toward the head of Murder Branch was a cave called Murder Cave. It got its name from back in the Indian days it was said

that a tribe of Indians captured some white women and took them back to the cave and murdered them. You could walk the first one hundred feet back in this cave and then you had to crawl the next fifty feet. Here you come out into a large room. From this there was a tunnel where you could crawl into the next room. There were seven of these rooms. I have been back in this cave.

On down the road was a sharp bend and the Widow Smith lived there with her two sons Vernon and Carl. Down from the Widow Smith's was a wooden bridge across Beaver. On the left past the bridge was a hillside with some trees. This was Buzzard Roost. There would be hundreds of buzzards roost there every night.

On down the road, if you look over to your right, up between the two mountains, you can see another mountain pretty far off. On this mountain, you can see a large square rock fifty feet or higher, with a bowl like rounded out space on the top. It is said that this stayes filled with water, and the buzzards come here to wash. So it is called Buzzards Wash. Us boys tried to climb up and see, but failed to climb it. I think it would take a cliff climber to get to the top.

On down the road we come to the Pat Montgomery family and Skidmore Creek. Up Skidmore lived the Louis Rose family and the John Sorrell family, also the Uncle Farm Wells family. Up at Uncle Farm's place there was a mountain with a large cave in shape of a barn. It was called Barn Cave. Uncle Farm kept his live stock in it.

Back down to the mouth of Skidmore, there was a branch that run off of Skidmore and run up between two mountains, and was called Soockey Branch. There lived the Lou Burns family. Lou was real old and nobody knew how old. She was called by everybody Aunt Soockey, and she lived up at the head of Soockey

Branch with her daughter Alice and Son-In-Law John Staton. They also had a young women staying with them that was retarded. Over aways from the mouth of Soockey Branch lived the Sherman Kring family. Sherman had a small country store. On down the road along Beaver, on the other side lived the Joe Charles family.

That reminds me of a little love affair between me and Ruby Charles. When we was going to school, I would write her letters and she would write me. Ruby was taking the letters from me and hiding them behind the dresser in her room.

One day her Mother was cleaning her room and found the letters and brought some of them and showed Pop and Mom. You talk about getting embarrassed, I was it. I guess my face was red enough to strike a match on. Ruby and I were just kids. There was a lane that separated our place and Grandpa Rollins. This lane went across Beaver to the Sadie Williams place. Courtney Williams lives there now. Back before I was born there had been a water mill at the lower end of our place and Beaver that run along our farm, called the Old Mill Dam. It was a long body of water wide and deep with no breaks intil at the upper end of our place was a ripple.

Of course, back across Beaver along the country road lived the Ginter family. On down at the mouth of Leatherwood creek lived Grandpa Rollings and on down a little ways was a road called

Leatherwood Road. At the corner of Beaver and Leatherwood Road was the Leatherwood school house.

Leading up the hill in front of the school was a rough road leading up to the Ginter Cemetery on top of Leatherwood Hill. Up Leatherwood the first family was the Ed Mynhier's. On up was the Henry Gillespie Family, next was the Ed Gillespie family, and the next was the Elbert and Henry Reed familys, and the last was the Proffit family that lived on Joe's Branch, which was a branch that run off Leatherwood.

Back down Leatherwood to Beaver Road, on down was the Winn Mynhier family on the other side of Beaver. Back over on the road side of Beaver, down a little ways lived the Ed Robinson family. This place was the Ginter's old home place. Down by the Robinson place was a lane that went across Beaver, and here lived the Newt Montgomery family. I went to school with the Montgomery kids.

One I remember real well was Hazel. When she had grown up she was courting my first cousin Herndon Sorrell. I always could tell when Herndon and Hazel was having a spat, because Herndon had to go past our house to go home, and if he was singing, "I'm going up this road a feelin bad, and I'm not going to be treated this away", I knew that they had disagreed on something.

On down the road was Johnson Holler. The widow Johnson and her sons Ben and Luther lived with her. Up the holler a little ways lived Henry Lee Robinson. Henry had a country store. None of these country stores had regular hours. You could go to the store and holler and the owner would come and open up. On down the road lived the Pritchard Johnson's.

Down farther was Buck Creek. At the mouth of Buck Creek was the Buck Creek school house. The was a road up Buck Creek and quite a few familys lived there, such as the Spencers, the Hunts, the Browns, and the Hiatts. Buck Creek community had all their social doings at the Buck Creek school house. On the road lived the Carpenter family, and on down was the Peach Donahue family, and next was the J.A Johnson family. Aunt Lou Johnson was mid-wife for the whole community. Next was the Crosswhite family. We are now getting into Bath County, and on down was Yale. Yale's buisness places were a general store, a post office, and a grist mill. Widow Caskey and her son Paul lived at Yale, and Mrs. Caskey was the post mistress. At the grist mill on Saturday was a busy day as it was mill day and every one come to Yale to get their corn meal ground and get their mail. There was a lot of horse trading going on this day. This is a run down on the familys that lived between Frenchburg and Yale. Beaver emptied into the Licking River just before you got to Yale.

Top: Pop, Walt, Mom. Bottom: Austin, Gma. Rollins, Adrian.

Author's Note:

Reflection of the Mountain Years in Menifee County

This concludes Chapter I of my story. The memories I've shared here are from a time and place that no longer exists, a world of hard work, close families, and neighbors who depended on each other for survival. Life in the mountains of Menifee County, Kentucky, in the 1920s was difficult, but it was also rich with community, adventure, and the kind of self-reliance that built character in ways that are hard to find today.

In the chapters to come, I will tell you about our move to Ohio during the Great Depression, and how our family adapted to a new life in a new place. But I wanted to start here, in these mountains, because this is where the Ginter family's story truly begins— where we learned the values and skills that would carry us through the hardest times America has ever known.

—-Ott Ginter

Chapter II

The Move To Dayton Ohio

1929-1952

The Journey to Ohio in Omar Gillespie's Buick

We were doing the routine of going hunting and etc. Then in 1929, Pop dropped a bombshell. He said we were going to have a sale and sell everything and move to Ohio. Pop had two brothers and some relation living in Ohio up around Miamisburg, Ohio and Pop said that is where we are going. Us boys thought that would be a great adventure for us because we hadn't traveled or been out of the mountains.

Come the time when we had the sale and sold everything, and that night we split up and stayed all night with relatives and I stayed with Aunt Monnie and Uncle Clay Whitt up on the old Bouldin place. We all met the next morning back at the house. Pop had hired Omar Gillespie and his big ole Buick touring car to take us to Ohio. We all climbed in that car and I don't know how we did it because there were seven of us kids and Pop and Mom and Omar the driver. That made ten people. We was on our way to Ohio. Us boys had two dogs that our Uncle said he would take and keep. Those two dogs run and followed us till they gave out and couldn't run anymore. That still pains me till this day.

Mom made up a lunch, and we stopped at a place where we could park and eat. It was by a cement wall of some kind. We then moved on and us kids was having a ball seeing things that we had never seen.

First Days in Miamisburg

Pop Begins Working in the Depression Years

We finally arrived in Miamisburg. Uncle Bill Ginter, Pop's brother, lived on a farm west of Miamisburg, so we went there. The family kinda split up for a few days till Pop could get located. I know Walter and me stayed at Uncle Bill's. The next day we helped Uncle Bill work on the farm, a old Kentucky tradition. If you stayed with someone, you helped him to do whatever was to be done. In a couple days, Pop come out to Uncle Bill's and got us and said he had rented a house downtown in Miamisburg at 802 E. Scymore St. and bought furniture and stocked up on food and moved in. We had electricity, running water, and a bathroom, and a coal furnace heating. This was all new to an ole Kentucky mountain family. At this time we started living in Ohio.

After moving in on 802 E. Scymore St., we started to get acquainted. Across the alley on our side of the street lived the McGowan's. They had two daughters, Daisy and Jewel. They were Mrs. McGowan's daughters. Down the street lived the Metcalfs, and up the street lived two familys of Ridinger's.

Down on the other side lived the Thompson's. They had three boys, Farris, Charlie, and Chester. Down farther lived the Williams, Across the street lived Harley Hennings. Well, Pop said, "I've got to get a job as I am running low on money." I think Pop was a brave man to leave the mountains with a family of nine when a depression was hitting. Well, Pop got a job with a fellow by the name of Casey Whitaker helping haul coal. Pop worked at this awhile. Then he found out that a distance relative by the name Auther Sorrell was a supervisor at the Loose Wiles Biscuit Company on Cincinnati St. in Dayton, and Art give him a job and Pop worked there all through the depression of the Thirties.

Pop and Mom at 802 Sycmore St.

Not long after we moved to Scymore Street, that one evening while we were eating supper Pop said, "One of you boys has to go back to Kentucky and help Grandpa Rollins put in his crop." And Pop looked straight at me, and I said, "Alright, I'll go." So that settled that. After a couple days, Pop bought me a ticket on a bus and I was on my way back down home in Kentucky. The bus stopped in Cincinnati and a pretty girl got on. She was sitting across the aisle from me. I smiled at her and she smiled back. Little later I winked at her and she returned the wink.

Remember, I was only fourteen years old but big enough for a eighteen year old. I didn't know anything about girls. Never did get up the nerve to talk to her. The bus stopped in Lexington Kentucky, and she got off. "Oh well," I said to myself, "and I didn't get her name. Well, I'll never see her again anyway." So my bus went on to Frenchburg. That was the end of the line. It was about fifteen miles down Beaver to Grandpa and Grandma's so I started walking. A man come along in a wagon and give me a ride for about eight miles, then I walked the rest of the way. When I got to Grandpa's I could see there was a light in the school house. Then I remembered this was Wednesday and prayer meeting night.

So I walked over to the school house. I didn't go in, but went around to a side window and looked in to see who was there. Lo and behold, sitting by the window was the girl that got off the bus in Lexington, so I got up enough nerve to talk to her through the window. I asked her, " May I walk you home after church." And she said yes. I didn't have any idea where she lived or was staying. After church I got her by the arm and we started walking up Leatherwood. She said her folks lived over on Buckcreek and she had walked with her folks across the mountain.

Meeting Maude Spencer and Dry Ridge Adventures

It was a old tradition that when a fellow got a new girl, it was up to the other fellows to try and take her away from him. The thing was when you were walking, the fellow would come up on the other side of her and ask to beat your time. And if she said yes, then you turned back. If she said no, then you went on. Three fellows tried to beat my time. Before I got back across that mountain that night I wished that one of them had, because it was a dark night but I got back to Grandpa's with only a few scratches and a few torn places in my clothes. The girls name was Maude Spencer. She said she was going out on Dry Ridge over the week end at her brothers. She wanted to

know if I was coming up on Sunday. I said I didn't think so because I didn't know where her brother lived. She tried to tell me how to get there. Well, I said, "I don't know, for I am not that familiar with Dry Ridge.

I was telling Grandpa about my events with this girl. He got a big kick out of it and went Ha! Ha!. He said you go up Sunday and ride ole Jake. Grandpa had a pair of real big mules, and I think Jake was the biggest. So early Sunday morning I saddled ole Jake and started out to go upon Dry Ridge. I came to Brushey, Maude said I could take a shot there. Well, I turned up Brushey and it was only a walking path, but the mule could walk in it O.K. I went a few miles and I couldn't see a path anymore but I kept on going, and pretty soon I said to myself, "By golly, I'm lost." Pretty soon I saw a house down in a holler. So I goe's down there to get directions and the man said, "You are sure enough lost for Dry ridge is over that way.", and he pointed. Now he says, "You can go back the way you come, or go through my corn crib over there, and it is not very far." So I said O.K. and I was leading ole Jake over to go through the corn crib, and the crib was too low and ole Jake couldn't get through. The man make a suggestion that we take the saddle off and maybe we could get through. Well by golly we just got through. Well, I went on and found her brothers house. Here I run into trouble again, for she had went to a dance Saturday nite and met another boy and he was there to see her. She explained that I hadn't said I was coming up Sunday.

Well, me and this fellow went outside to talk it over who would stay. He was packing a gun, and said, "We will shoot at some marks and the winner stays." I said O.K. and we started shooting at some bottles. Her brother comes out and said, "Boys, I don't allow no shooting here on Sunday." He had a rifle in his hands. We said O.K. and we apologize. He said dinner is ready. You all come to dinner. Well, we eat dinner and I said I wasn't going to be in Menifee County very long, that I was going back to Ohio, and I would go and he could stay. I never saw Maude Spencer again.

Helping Grandpa and going fishing

Well, I got back into the swing of things helping Grandpa get his crop out. Grandpa was a big kidder. Every morning he would come into my room and holler as loud as he could, and jump in bed on top of me. He was a big man. One other time me and a niece by the name of Burl Whitt was staying at Grandpa's. She would go fishing with me. Well, one day Grandpa said, "I am going with you fellows and show you how to catch some fish." This really was an honor for Grandpa didn't go fishing with no one. Well, me him, and Burl went fishing. We Baited our hooks and throwed out in the water, and I caught a little minnow. I left it on my hook and cast out again. That ole line had no more than hit the water. It was grabbed and I had a hard time pulling it in. It was a thirty inch catfish. Grandpa looked at me and said, "I'm going back to the house." That was the last time I got to go fishing with Grandpa. I don't think he went fishing with anyone again.

Burl Whitt was the daughter of Aunt Monnie, the daughter of Grandpa's. So Grandpa Rollins was Burl's Grandpa too. Burl was only a young girl but she tagged after me every place I went. If I took the wagon to haul something Burl was right there ready to go. Aunt Lacey and Brock Lovelace come down to visit Grandpa and

Grandma's. Lacey was one of Grandpa and Grandma's daughter. Pop had told them if Grandpa's crop was in to bring me back to Ohio with them.

Well, me and Grandpa had all of his crop in, so I come back to Ohio with them. I didn't want to for I was homesick to stay in Kentucky, but I come back.

I was back home on Scymore St. I started to get acquainted with the neighborhood boys. Faris Thompson on the other side of the street. His family was from down home on Beaver. I got acquainted with a fellow by the name of Elmer Clark, and one by the name of Arthur White, and Harley Hennings. Aunt Lacey and Uncle Brock Lovelace stopped by one Sunday and said they were going I said to Walter, "Why don't we ask Uncle Brack if he would give us a ride to Indinia." And he said yes. So me and Walter went to Huntertown Indinia. Next morning we went over to Ort & Company and applied for a job. They gave Walter a job right away at $18.00 a week. But they questioned me about my age. I had to lie a little bit and tell them I was 16. I was only fifteen. They finally gave me a job at $15.00 a week because of my age of sixteen. Uncle took us to work on Monday. Paul Gilauhm was the over see'r of the onion fields. Paul had a teenage daughter by the name of Virginia and she had a Chevy car and said she would take us home after quitting time. She did. She said she would pick us up in the morning and take us to work. I told Walter Virginia must have fell for him the way she was shinning up and taking us to and from work. Well, I found out later that it wasn't Walter, it was me she was shinning up to. There was a carnival going on in Churubusco and she asked me to go with her. I took her to the carnival or she took me, and to a couple of ball games.

Working the Onion Fields in Indinia

At that time we were getting board and washing for $5.00 a week. Hunterstown was located in Allen County, and where they raised onions was muck land. The saying was that thousands of years ago it had been lakes. All kinds of onions was raised here and all from seeds. The big sweet onion to the little pickler. Of course they raised other things such as peppermint, potatoes, corn. Corn was generally planted in between sections of onions for wind-break, to keep the wind from blowing the onions out of the ground. This muck ground is that loose. It will burn, not blaze, but smother. You cannot use a tractor with wheels, one spin and the tracter is stalled. You can use half track caterpillars. If corn is not planted for windbreak then you would have to build one out of burlap.

We worked till the growing season was over, then we worked in the dry shed grading onions. It took six men to run this grader. The grader is made of wood, with different size sections. One man would load the rack and two first men, on each side, would agitate them and hulls and dirt would fall through to a retaining trash box. The onions were pushed down to the next two men and they would agitate them and the small ones would fall through to a container.

That left the large onions on top. They were pushed out the end of the grader into shipping bags. Sized bags was scheduled for that day and loaded into box cars for shipping. One day while grading onions I got into a wrestling match with one of the men and he had a toe hold on me and was hurting me real bad, when gold ole Walter come over and pulled him off.

We worked there in the dry shed for about a month, and one morning Walter said, "Let's go home back to Ohio." We then went to the boss and got our money and walked to the train station and got our tickets. Then we went back to Uncle Ernest's where we were boarding and got our belongings and left on the evening train.

Back to Dayton

We arrived in Dayton Ohio, then we had to get a traction car to Miamisburg. We didn't know where to catch the traction car. A man came to us and ask us where we was going. We told him we had to catch a car to Miamisburg. He said come with me and I'll show you. We went with him and we boarded a city trolley. I said to Walter, "Something is wrong. We are on a city bus.' He said, "I guess so.", so we got off at the next block, and went and asked a news stand where to catch the car. He told us and we got to Miamisburg alright without a mugging. That's what we think that that man was up to.

Wasn't long till school would start so I went down and registered. So I started to school at Miamisburg High. I was a junior, right from the first. I couldn't make any friends. None of the girls and boys would talk to me. Pretty soon I noticed that the teachers seem to avoid me. I found out later what the trouble was. The word got out that not to have any thing to do with me. That I was a Kentucky hill billy and carried a big knife to leave me alone. This was all a big lie. The teachers treated me the same way. All the time I went to school the teachers didn't give me one assignment, not one. When I first started we changed rooms for every class. Teachers wouldn't tell me what room the next class would be in. I had to go from room to room intil I found the right one. After so long of time being ignored by class mates and teachers, I said this school is not for me, so I told the superintendent a lie about my age. I told him I was sixteen when I was only fifteen, and I wanted a work permit, that I was dropping out of school. He didn't give me any trouble. I guess he felt the same as the rest of the school. When I went home and told Mom she really read the riot act to me. She had hopes of me getting a good education. Pop, he didn't say much. I guess he thought Mom had said it all.

That summer me and Raymond went over in Indinia to work the onion fields to get work. Work was slowing down in the onion growing and we could only get work three and four days a week. After a few weeks we came home. Raymond got a job at a furniture factory in Miamisburg. He worked there till they shut down for lack of business. The depression had started to show up and taking effect. Factory's shutting down. Workers getting layed off. But Pop was still working at the biscuit company. In fact, he worked there all during the depression.

Farming During the Depression

Sorghum-Making and the Crowds Who Came to Watch

Pop was a pretty smart cookie. He rented a small farm. I think it was about seventeen acres, and borrowed enough money to buy a team of horses and some farming equipment. And he kept on working and put us boys to farming. I guess the old Kentucky farming was hard to get out of our system. Because the first year we raised sugar cane to make sorghum mollases. This kind of a crop was very few in Ohio, but we located a man who had a outfit of sorghum making equipment, so we contracted to use it. Our little farm faced Hienke Road on one side, but on the other side it was only a few yards from Twelveth Street and the city limits of Miamisburg. There was a walking place from our place to Twelveth Street.

When sorghum making time come, we sent to Kentucky and got a fellow by the name of Little Joe Sorrell, who was an expert in making sorghum. It took us about a week to make the mollases. Like I said, we were close to town. In the evenings, it was like a circus at the cane mill. People coming from town and other towns to watch us make sorghum. It was something they had never seen before. From the crowds, you would think it was a tourist place. It was during the depression, but Pop sold all of that sorghum mollases for $1.25 a gallon, and that was top price.

Growing the Family Farm in the 1930s

Pop was still a wise ole duck. He got hold of a hundred and eighty acre farm & bought a pair of mules, so that made two teams to farm with. There was two houses on the farm. By this time Raymond was married and he moved in the tennant house. After the first year, we started putting everything we could into live stock. We built our live stock up to eight milk cows, thirty five young cattle, three hundred young and old hogs, and Mom raised a thousand chickens. This was in three to four years into the depression. In nineteen thirty three, we bought a farm-all tractor and later on a one row corn picker. With Pop still working and selling cream, eggs, and pork, and farm produce when we could, we had a pretty good income coming in. Not a huge one but more than most. It was enough that we were living above average for those days.

Youth, Dating, and Getting Married

I was still going to Miamisburg and running around with my old gang. We got to hanging around the Holiness Church, mostly to meet girls. I was walking up the street one night up from the church, where I met a fellow walking up the street with two women. I was walking along talking to him when his girlfriend said, " Why don't you walk with her." She was meaning the other woman. I walked with her. We walked the women home that night . They lived about two miles out of town on Gebhart Church Road which was west of Miamisburg. I made a date for the next night. Then I found out she had been married and had some children. She was 27 years old and I was an ole mountain boy, only seventeen years old, and didn't know any thing about women. Her name was Velma Branscomb and she was staying with her sister-in-law, who was a widow woman. I dated her for quite a while, then I quit dating her for a long time.

Then one day a car pulled in our drive-way with what I thought was a lone male, but when I got over to the car Velma raised up from hiding, and she said they were having a little party Saturday nite and would I come. I said maybe I'll drop by which I did and I started dating her again. As I was a ole dumb mountain boy with no experience at all what life is about. She was experienced and had me dominated from the start. After a while I got to neglecting my work on the farm. Her sister-in-law had a building out from her house, it had a cot in it. It was about six miles from our house to theirs and the only way I had of getting there was walking. So I started sleeping in the out building and was going home on the week-end.

The other boys didn't like it, but I thought three of them was enough to run the farm. She was promising me a lot of things and giving me sex. You see, she was in charge. Right after my nineteenth birthday, she talked me into marrying her, so we got married. It was the hardest thing in my life telling Mom. I went home and Mom was out in the corn field getting some roasting ears. I knowed that Mom was not going to approve it, but when I told her she shed a few tears, and said bring her on home. Well, I did and we stayed there on the farm intill 1935. I decided to go out on my own. My thinking was, if Pop could do it at the beginning of the depression with seven children, just why couldn't I do it.

I thought there were enough boys on the farm to handle the farming. There was Raymond, Walter, and Austin, and Adrian was getting big enough to help. So we left and I didn't have a job. But Mamie, who Velma had stayed with, said we could move in the out building. It only had one large room, but she promised us that if I would build on to it, we could live there as long as we wanted to.

At first I got a job working in Charlie Baver's grocery store. I would get paid in grocerys, then I would pick up a days work here and there, maybe one day a month at a paper mill, working on a ice route when a worker was absent. A day or two shoveling sand, unloading box cars at the foundry in Miamisburg. The depression was getting worse and a days work was hard to find. Finally, I signed up for welfare. It was O.K., but I kinda held off getting a little work to keep us going. Then W.P.A. come along and I signed up and I was given a job making $50.00 a month. We worked forty hours a week on W.P.A. We bought and was given enough furniture to furnish the one room. I decided to build on. I goes down to Owen Gross Lumber Company and I tell Mr. Gross what I wanted to do and I needed some lumber. I didn't have any money, but I could pay him so much every month. He let me have the lumber just on a hand shake, no papers signed on or anything. I then built on to the building, and we had a pretty nice little place.

Mamie was a widow. Her husband had got killed in a accident with a Dayton Power and Light truck, and was awarded some money from the Dayton Power and Light company. We had lived there awhile when Emmit Branscomb, her brother-in-law was her guardian and he didn't like me, so he told Mamie that I would have to start paying rent. She come and told me what Emmit said and that I would have to. I told her that was not our agreement, and I wasn't about to pay her rent when she had agreed to let us live there for the building I had done. So I went over on Union Road and bought a acre of land off of Charles Chatten.

The cost for the acre of land was $150.00. I didn't have that much money, so I made a deal with Corless Grushon to take the back half. I dug a well on the front half, and built a large one room house. Charlie Baver give me most of the lumber to build it. Before Charlie went into the grocery business he did carptner work and had a lot of lumber that he had not used.

I worked for awhile for the W.P.A. Then I got a job with the Zehring Hurst Dairy Company for $15.00 a week, so I quit the W.P.A. working forty hours a week at $12.50 a week and went to a daily working sixty hours a week for $15.00 Anyway I was off public works.

I kept thinking about Pop and Mom out there on the farm going along as if there was no depression, and me out here a struggling, when I could have been out there with them. Oh well, I would have had to start sometime. Things were pretty cheap in those days. Bread five cents a loaf, eggs ten cents a dozen, cigarettes ten cents a pack, shoes $1.98 a pair, gasoline twelve and fourteen cents a gallon. I bought a good Model A Ford for $65.00. Of course I had to save a long time to get the sixty five dollars.

In the early thirties at the start of the depression, we elected a new President Franklin D Roosevelt. First thing he closed all the banks for a day and re-organized them. Unemployment was sky high and soup lines were every where. Then the President declared a new deal and started the NRA-National Recovery Administration. And from this the Works Progress Administration-WPA. This put needy unemployed to work starting at $50.00 a month. You could live on this in those times. You worked for what you got. It was not handed out free. There were a lot of jokes about WPA, but I worked on it a little while and I tell you it wasn't any joke. It was very productive, some of the good it did was small rural towns got sewer lines, some got new schools built, new municipal buildings, golf courses, and a lot more building. The counties got bridges replaced, country road ditches cleaned and new culberts, and I could go on and on the good things were done.

Changing Jobs and Home Troubles

Like I said, I got off the W.P.A. as soon as I found another job, which was with a dairy. My marriage hadn't got any better. I guess it was the difference in our ages. Velma was ten years older than me, I guess she thought I was too young to make family decisions. She was dominating. She wanted to rule the roost and I hadn't no say. I had to bring my pay check home and she would go get it cashed. I couldn't go anywhere by myself. We finally come to the conclusion that our marriage was a mistake. We didn't hate one another, nothing like that. I didn't want to leave at that time and neither did she, so we just let things go on as usual.

In Nineteen Thirty Seven I put in an applician at Delco Brake GMC for a job. I put on my applician that I had no experience working in a factory but one thing I did know and that was how to work. I worked at Delco Brake, but got layed off at the end of the year. In the meanwhile I had bought another acre of land from Mr. Chatten joining my current land and had started to build a bigger and better house. Velma's father owned and operated a sawmill and he sold me the lumber real cheap. It was all oak outside of the siding, it was poplar.

Well, Pop was still out on the farm, but two of the boys had left to go on their own, and Pop was looking for a smaller farm. I went to work back at Delco Brake, but in the forties I got laid off again.

GM was changing over their machinery to make lend lease war material for England.

After getting layed off, I got a job at the Oxford Miami paper mill in West Carrollton. I worked there for awhile and Delco called me back to work. I contacted them but did not take the job they offered me. I stayed with the paper mill.

One day my neighbor wanted me to drive him to Dayton to look for a job. I took him to Leland Electric, and I got in line talking to him, I'll be darned if they didn't give me a job, and I took it and went back to the paper mill and quit. By this time I was thinking about education or a skilled trade, so I took a course in the complete field of electricity, and a course in radio.

I had a good easy job at Leland on final inspection, but I didn't like it to well. I finished building my new house and then I decided to quit Leland Electric. You might say I was prospecting around. I got a job with United Aircraft making airplane coolers. Leland Electric kept calling me, wanting me to come back to work for them. Finally, I quit United Aircraft and went back to Leland Electric, but I didn't like it any better, so I give them notice that I was quitting. With me background of electric they wanted me to stay, offered me more money, and offered me a job in the lab, but I guess the old Ginter stubbornness kept me from changing my mind.

One day I walked in the employment office at Delco Brake and Bob Maines the employment manager said Ott, I got a job for you down at Moraine Products. I knew Bob and he didn't give me a chance to ask him for a job. They had built this new factory right below Delco Brake and called it Moraine Products, division of GMC. They made parts from powdered metal.

It was fascination work to see all kinds of bushings and gears and many more products pressed to form out of powder metal copper, and iron, and run through a production furnace and come out most of the time a finished product. After working at Moraine Products a while, I bought a radio and electric shop on East Fifth Street in Dayton, but I kept on working at Moraine Products, and run the shop on the side. The name of the shop was The East End Radio and Electric Shop.

We started going to 50-50 dances. That was square dancing and round dancing. The dance hall was owned and operated by Bob McRose and Johnny Gunthlan. I got to know them pretty well, and they hired me to give free square dance lessons to their patrons on Saturday Nite before the dance. After awhile Johnny said to me if you will call a square dance, I will. We both called a dance. We didn't do real well, but passable. From there on we would call a square dance at least once a week. Pretty soon we were professional square dance callers. So I started calling dances at different places on Wednesday, Saturday, and Sunday nites. This give me another part time job to make some money, and didn't interfere with my other work.

Pretty soon, I was a well known square dance caller through out the territory, and was swamped with calls to call square dances.

During the war I had a ration amount of copper to use on electric repair, but could not get anything on radio parts, so it was harder and harder to get parts, especially radio tubes. So I sold my radio and electric business and went to the rationing board and applied for more pounds of copper per month, for electric wire to do electric contract work, and they granted it. So I started another part time job. The next project was I heard that Right Patterson Field wanted airplane tube welders, and was paying top price. So I go to the Tri-State welding company and take a welding course, including airplane tube welding. I never tried to get a job at Right Pat., as I was satisfied where I was. I was thinking my best potential was with GM, so I stayed.

Pop quits farming and Moves to Dayton

Well, Pop got out of the farming business, as all the boys had went out on their own. He bought some property on Taylor Street in Dayton. Him and Mom lived there for awhile. Then they bought a double on Webster Street in Dayton. Pop come to me and asked could I build on to the Taylor Street house and make for renting furnished rooms and apartments. I told him I would try to run it into my schedule. I hired Austin's brother-in-law to help me. It took all summer long to do it part time to finish it. When we got finished, Pop had four furnished rooms and one furnished apartment on Taylor Street, and one half of a double of six rooms on Webster Street to rent. Pop wasn't fooling me. With the money he made at farming, and these rental properties, plus what he would get from retireing from the Sunshine Biscuit Co., he would have a good substantial income for the rest of his and Mom's life. Pretty good for a man with nine in the family, coming from the mountains in the time of the great depression in the thirties. Brother Walter went to Michigan and went to work in a General Motors plant. Raymond worked in various places until in the forties, he was drafted into the Army. Austin was also in the Army and Adrian in the Navy. When the boys got out of the service, Raymond and Austin went to work as home improvement contractors, installing aluminum products, siding, windows, doors, and awnings. Also a brother-in-law Bud Baker, Marie's husband, worked with them.

Setting Up a Business After the War

We were visiting Pop and Mom one Sunday and all the boys were there. They were talking, saying they would like to start their own company of furnishing the public with this complete service. I made them a proposal that I would set them up a company and manage it for six months and then turn it over to them. The company would belong to Raymond, Austin, Adrian, and Bud Baker, the brother-in-law.

73

They said go ahead and set the company up. I got finance companies and banks to take the credit loans and within two weeks I had the company set up and ready to go. I rented office space on E. Fifth Street in Dayton, and hired a secretary, and the siding and roofing company R&S was in business. Here I run into another obstacle. With all the activity going on at the office, Velma forbid me to go to the office without her. Well, this widened the gap of our relations some more. It went on for quite awhile and the company was making money, I was getting so hard a time about the business that I turned it over to the boys before the six months were up.

Raymond and Austin finally dropped out giving the company to Adrian and Bud. They exspanded and bought a laundry as a add on to the company.

They operated the company for some time and all at once they closed the company. I never did know why. Adrian and Bud went to work as salesmen for The Dayton Roof and Remodeling Company, Inc. Austin went back to work installing siding and windows and doors.

Starting a Band and The Osborne Brothers

I never went back to my part time electrical business. As a side job I was calling square dances. I owned a guitar and had learned to pick it a little, and also had a wire recorder. My next door neighbor played the guitar. He would come over and we would fool around recording. He said I got a nephew that is real good on playing lead guitar and he had a good voice. He brought his nephew over and his name was Bobby Osborne.

At that time Bobby was 15 years old, and that is how I met Bobby Osborne. Bobby started to come often and we would have jam sessions. He started bringing a cousin of his by the name of Clarence Collett, who was a good rythem guitar player. Spellman a piano player, Kenny Seiple drummer and R. Webb played the fiddle. We were doing pretty good, but was taking up too much of my time, so I finally disbanded the band.

I knew a disk jockey by the name of Tommy Sutton. We recorded and made some records and Tommy would play them over WONE. Also I knew Ranny Daily, manager of radio station WPFB in Middletown. I got Bobby a job on a early morning program. I would go with Bobby sometimes and play the Jews harp, a solo on the program. They later on were having a talent show and bringing in big time bluegrass and country music bands, and I got Bobby a job playing at the tent show. After that the station hired Bobby to go out and play with their band. Of course I would take Bobby to the station and pick him up at night. Pretty soon a fellow came along by the name of Larry Richardson, who played a banjo. Him and bobby went to Bluefield West Virginia. They got a job playing with the Lonesome Pine Fiddlers, playing over W.H.I.S. radio. I went down and stayed two weeks with Bobby to kinda see how he was doing. Bobby kept in touch from time to time.

Later, I got a call from Bobby saying him and Larry had a contract with Cozy Record Company to cut a record and wanted to know if they could use one of the songs that I had wrote. The name of the song was "Pain In My Heart". Later on it was picked up by Mercury records and put out with Earl Scruggs and Lester Flatt as the recording artists. Bobby finally come back home, as his family lived on Oakes Road about three miles from Union Road where I lived.

Bobby did not bring Larry Richardson back with him. In the meanwhile, Sonny, Bobby's younger brother had learned to pick a five string banjo and he was real good at it. Later on Bobby and Sonny teamed up and called themselves the Osborne Brothers. For quite awhile they played in the area, mostly at nite clubs, but wasn't getting anything big, but was very popular in this area. Then Tommy Sutton, the disk

jockey, took them to Nashville and introduced them to a recording studio. He knew the people that run it and he got the boys a recording contract. After that they were known as recording artists, they began to appear at big time shows.

From then on they made the big time.

Bobby Osborne

Louise Osborne, Me, Sonny Osborne with the wire recorder

Working at Moraine Products During World War Two

During World War Two I was working at Moraine Products on essential war materials. Raymond was drafted and overseas, Austin was drafted and was serving in the States, and Adrian was drafted and was serving in the Navy in the South Pacific. Walter was working for GMC making essential war materials in a plant in Michigan. He got deferments.

I kept on working at Moraine Products. The service was taking the men as quick as we could hire them. I was a group leader and my job was to train these new people. Finally the company started hiring women. I had wondered why Uncle Sam hadn't called me. I found that Moraine Products was getting me deferments and I didn't know it intil they told me that the department would not need very much training as it was in good shape, and they would not be getting me any more deferments. In a few weeks I got notice to report to my draft board.

I was ordered to Columbus for an exam. I passed my exam and was suppose to be called in about two weeks. But before the two weeks were up, Japan surrendered and my draft board reclassified me and I was not called.

When I first hired in at Delco Brake, I was hired as a machine operator. By this time, Delco Brake had changed its name to Moraine Products. Next I was promoted to jobsetter and then I was promoted to group leader. Then in 1952, there was an opening on supervision in my department. The plant Supt. Norman Gebhart asked me if I wanted the job and I said yes. He said you've got it, and if you don't make it don't blame me.

Chapter III

Divorce and Re-Marriage

1953-1961

Meeting Florence Bowerman

I had got an excellent reputation as a square dance caller and I could work at it as many nights as I wanted to. I met a woman at one of these dances. She was in the process of getting a divorce. We got pretty well aquainted, and I fell in love with her and she said she loved me, and I believed her.

We let it ride for awhile then one day I asked Velma for a divorce. Well she had changed her mind and said no. The woman's name was Florence Evelyn Bowerman. I started to seeing her pretty often. Velma knew this for one day she left a note in my glove compartment sayins I hoped you enjoyed that woman.

Florence had gotten her divorce, and I talked some more with Velma and she said she would think about it. I waited quite awhile and approached her again and she said no. Well later on she said if I give her the home and the bank account and a car and paid her so much a month up until and if she got married again. I drew up a paper agreeing to all these things but I never did tell Florence what I had to give away to get a divorce. The payment run a long time for Velma didn't get married again. Me and Florence got married and out first child was born May 18th 1954.

Randolph's Birth and Our Early Family Life

Our first born was a boy and we named him Randolph Eugene. He was about two years old when Florence's Father and Mother come to live with us. That old saying that you can't get along with your mother-in-law is all bull. They were superb people and we were lucky to have them living with us. When Randolph was about seven his sister Lori Carleen was borned. Randolph was jealous and couldn't understand why he was not getting all of our attention. We tried to tell him that he now had a little sister and we loved him as much as always but his little sister would get part of the attention that he had got all these years, that we loved them both.

I was still calling square dances and they were 50-50 dances. Half square dancing and half modern dancing. We started taking Randolph dancing with us when he was small by the time he was seven years old. He could hold his own with the best of the other dancers. Then we started taking Lori with us when Randolph was 12 and Lori 5. They made a good looking dance pair. They were able to square dance in any set.

Me Callin a Square Dance With R. Webb on Fiddle

Pop's Illnesses and Recovery

Losing Pop and Remembering His Life

One day I got a call from Mom saying Pop was on the way to the
hospital he had a stroke. He was supposed to be going to Good
Sam hospital. I went ther but Pop wasn't there, that they were full
up and sent him to St. E hospital. So I found him there. After a few
weeks Pop was sent home. He was partially paralyzed on one side.
That didn't faze Pop he said I'll recover from that. and he did.
Later on he had to had open heart surgery. Well ole Pop said I'm
going to get out of here, and he did. Later on they called me from
the shop and said Pop was

back in the hospital and the doctors said he wouldn't live more than twelve hours. This is about ten PM. I got over to the hospital and Pop was unconscious. I stayed with him and about three he regained conscious and said to me I guess they told you I was going to die, but I'm not. I'm getting out of here, and he did, but his health got worse and he passed away in 1971 at the age of 87.

Mom Ginter's Influence and Passing

Mom Ginter was the head of the Ginter clan. When Mom put her foot down everybody listened. Everybody in the clan went to Mom Ginter for advice. She kept in touch what was going on back in Kentucky. She was smart and a good manager.

She was proud of the out come of all the children. If Mom give you any advice you had better heed it because it would be like she said. In the later years Mom had to have gall bladder operation, and after that she got heart trouble, but she wouldn't give up. After a few years passed away at a good old ripe age of 96 in 1985.

Chapter IV

Starting A New Business & Moving to Pleasant Hill, Ohio

1962-1973

Helping Raymond and Austin with Home Improvement Work

Raymond and Austin were working as home improvement contractors. They were getting behind on their work and asked me if I would work part time and help them out. I said OK. I was working the second shift at Delco Moraine, and I could work probably four or five hours a day. That was alright with them, so I started working installing siding, doors, awnings, shutters, and any other things to be done.

Family Life and Vacations

There seemed to be a lot of work in this business, and Raymond and Austin were only sub-contractors. After about a year, I felt as I knew enough about home improvement that I could do it on my own. In the early sixties Florence and me and the kids were going to the Smokey Mountains on vacation.

Before we left I got a name for the company, and I put in an application to some banks so I could run credit applicants through them. When we returned from vacation, I had been OK'd by First National Bank to get personal and F.H.A. loans for my clients.

Starting the Ginter Aluminum Company

That was the starting of the Ginter Aluminum Company. I bought me a pickup truck and different sizes ladders and other tools that I needed. The only advertising I done was by mouth, of course when it was known at the shop, jobs started coming in. The first job I got I hired two men from the shop to work for me. They were two of the best men, Arvil Frost and James Edgar. They worked for me for a long time. Edgar got sick and couldn't work anymore. Frost worked for me fourteen years and then he decided to go to work for himself. Elmer Dunn worked for me some. Elmer was one of the good ole boys

Randolph Learns the Trade

Randolph was getting to be a good sized boy and I started taking him along to work with me and have him doing small things and cleaning up at the end of the days work.

Things were going along pretty good for the Ginter Aluminum Company. I was getting more work than three people could do, so I started looking for application crews. But people to do the quality work that I required where hard to find. I tried a few crew but they did not come up to my standards, so I kinda quit looking intil one day Raymond come to me and wanted to go to work for me. He had his son Kenneth helping him. He said the companies he had been working for wouldn't let him run the jobs the way they were supposed to be run and he didn't like that. Raymond was the type of fellow any job worth doing was worth doing right. He said I know you want your jobs run right, and Kenny and me would like to work for you.

I told him he could work for me but I didn't know if I could keep him busy in the winter time. He went to work for me, and this took the worries off me wether the jobs were being run right, because I knowed that Raymond would do a quality job on them.

Well Randolph was getting up there in age old enough to go to work so I put him working with Raymond. I kept Raymond busy for over twenty years intil he passed away in 1983. Back to when my company was young, I kept on working at Delco Moraine and also running my home improvement company.

My income was up and me & Florence had started saving some money and buy things we needed and go on vacations. We always took the kids everywhere with us.

Managing Another Country Music Singer

There was a fellow working at Delco Moraine who was trying to make it in country music and wanted me to help him. So I listened to him sing, and he did have a good voice and I told him I would be his manager for awhile and we would see what happens. We first started recording him singing then we would go over it and review it. We did this for about a month. Then I started to get him some interviews with some record

people and disc jockeys. I got aquainted with a disc jockey by the name of Griffin Oat in Lancaster Kentucky. Kenny Long was my singer's name. Me and Kenny organized a band to play with Kenny.

Recordings, Radio Shows, and Television Appearances

Or first job was in Corbin Kentucky on the radio at a huge housing project opening. We cut two songs on Spinner Records in Columbus Ohio. She got us an appearance on television in Parkersburg West Virginia. We had some bad luck with this company. The owner had got some distributors for the record and had got us personal appearances on T.V. shows, intill all at once the owner got sick and died in a short time with cancer. That was the end of Spinner Records. No one took over the company.

Then we cut two songs on Camaro Records in Memphis Tenn. Next we had a one hour spot on a country show at a theater in Broadhead Kentucky. Next we performed on Channel 22 in Dayton Ohio for close to twelve weeks. We also was on the Saturday night show in Renfro Valley in Kentucky. At the time it was owned by John Lair. John told me that we could come back anytime, I didn't need to call him, just come down and he would have a spot on the show.

We was also on WPFB radio station in Middletown Ohio for six weeks. I didn't have the time to follow up on the Camaro label, as I was working at Delco Moraine and also running Ginter Aluminum Company.

Some of the fellows at the shop got with me and wanted to have a country show. We took up a collection and rented a hall. We had country music, square dancing, modern dancing, soft drinks, eats. Everything was free, all performers volunteered their time. We had one of these every three months. They were a big sucess .

Searching for a Home in the Country

Buying and Renovating the Shiloh Road Home

In 1968 Florence and me we would like a home in the country. I was so busy the looking was left up to Florence. The first one she found was in Pitsburg Ohio, and I went along with her to look at it. We liked it, but another couple had first chance to buy it, so Florence kept on looking. Next she found one in New Paris Ohio. I went with her to check it out. It was not exactly what we were looking for and it was pretty far from my work. Next she found this house on Shiloh Road near Pleasant Hill Ohio. So we went up to check it out, and we liked it pretty well. She called the Real Estate to find out what price they wanted. He told me and I made him a counter offer. I didn't hear from the real estate man after a couple weeks went by, so I called him up and give him the highest price I would pay for it, and he said he would present it to the owner. In a few days he called me back and said the owner accepted the offer.

Life in Pleasant Hill and Gardening

So we bought the house on Shiloh Road near Pleasant Hill. It had with it three acres of ground, a bank barn and a tobacco barn with an outbuilding size twelve by twenty four and a milk cooler house about ten by twelve. A real nice garden spot with plenty of room to expand. Randolph and Lori wanted to come out and see our new home.

Coming our Range Line Road I came to an old house that had been abanded and was falling down, so I stopped and said to the kids this is it. Well their eyes got big and round, but Florence could not keep from laughter and then the children knowed it was a joke.

The owner had remodeled part of the house, so I took four weeks vacation and finished remodeling. So in sixty nine we moved in and Florence had never lived in the country but she sure loved it out here.

Well we started going back to 50-50 dances and taking vacations in Tenn. and sometimes visited my home place in Kentucky. We always took the kids with us. We would visit Florence's cousins Charlie and Colleen Thomas in Virginia, also my cousin Haskel

Stamper in Logan, West Virginia, and friends Bob Raulston and Beau, and Bill and Hatty Colter in South Pittsburg Tenn.

At our new home on Shiloh Road, First year I put a big garden. I had a

bumper crop of vegetables, like potatoes, beans, corn, tomatoes, cabbage, lettuce, cucumbers, onions, bell peppers, and other things. I had a asparagus that was 10 by 30 feet and started a strawberry patch that was 3 rows about 30 feet each row. I can tell you that Florence loved every minute of living in the country. I was having some problems at Delco Moraine. For the last years they had been trying to promote me to the highest level of supervision. I always turned them down. I felt with my education I could handle a couple steps higher, but above that was a question.

I more or less solved the problem myself, as I had a good reputation as a foreman and had the name of getting things done. In powered metal, I felt pretty secure in my job at Delco Moraine. With my aluminum company, I was making more money than I could get at a higher level.

We went to school so many hours a week. GM would send GMI teachers down to our plant to continue the classes. They kept on giving us tests or grades. I got so I would answer enough questions to give me a passing grade. I know this wasn't right. I felt like this was cheating, but again I have to look out for my own security. The way I thought was when it came to retirement time, with my retirement income from the shop and I would operate my aluminum company for awhile and then my retirement would be secure.

Chapter V

Retirement

1974-1995

Adjusting to Home Life After 30 Years on Second Shift

A few years later my chance to retire with full benefits came. I was in my department about 5 o'clock in 1974 when the personal manager came down the aisle and hollered, I have some news that you might like. I just got news from Detroit. Anyone that's 55 years old and with 30 years service can retire with full benefits. I said is the salary supervisor still here. We went to personal and he was. I signed up and left at 11:00. I called Florence and said when do you want me to retire., and she said as quick as you can. I said how about tonight. She didn't believe me intill I got home. I thought I'll have my retirement from GM, my home improvement, and later on my social security. That sounded good to me, taking my vacation on to my retirement. That made it Jan. 1974 when I retired.

Running the Home Improvement Company Full

Time Managing Finances with Stock and Savings

I had belonged to the stock purchase program since it started in 1955. I recieved my stock when I retired. I didn't do much the rest of that year, just stayed around home and enjoyed being with the family. I had worked over thirty years on second shift and beside that, the last few years I took care of my home improvement company. So I was from home a lot and I was enjoying being home. Well the next year I started putting full time in running my home improvement company. I was pretty busy that year which was 1975. I go together with Florence and went over what we owed and tried to find a way to pay them off.

Finally we come up with a total. Then we figured how much our stock was worth. We figured that we could sell some of them and pay off all our bills and have money left over. Our next problem was what we wanted to do with the rest of the money. After thinking awhile we decided to buy a new car, as I was getting 25% off from GM. We decided to buy a Cadillac. So, in '76 I went over to the plant and ordered one, a "77 model. Really I wanted it for Florence to drive. Late in "76 it arrived and it sure was a pretty thing. Florence was thrilled. First trip we took was down on Beaver in Kentucky.

Beginning a Life of Travel Trips with Adrian and Wanda

My brother Adrian had been bugging me for years to go on a trip with him and Wanda. They had been going on trips for a few years to the Virgin Islands, Mexico, and other places. He finally talked me and Florence going with them on a cruise. I always said I wouldn't fly on a plane and Florence had always said she wouldn't go on a ship. She was afraid of the water. You know we flew to Florida and got on the ship and went on a cruise. We really enjoyed the trip. We went to Porta-Plata in the Dominican Republic. It had just opened to tourists. From there we went to Puerto Rico. From there we went to St. Thomas and on to Nassau. That ended our first trip. But more trips coming up.

Expanding the Business and Traveling

Cruises, Caribbean Adventures, and Las Vegas Trips

Next we went to Las Vegas with Adrian and Wanda for three days and 4 nights. We stayed at the Imperial Palace Casino and Hotel. Florence really liked thos quarter poker machines. If I wanted to find her, all I had to do was go to the poker machines and there she was. For her to find me was to start at the dollar machines. If I wasn't there, then check the quarter machines, then check the nickel machines. It was how my luck was going that day would determined as to what machines I would be at. That brother Adrian was the luckiest man I ever saw playing the slot machines. I'd lose my shirt and he always came away a winner.

Adrian owned a home improvement co., but he was big time. He had ten to twelve crews working for him, and his gross sales were over a million dollars each year. Adrian made me a proposal that I couldn't turn down. He has a space in his office. The proposal was that I move my office in this space, and he would have his secretary answer my phones and he would pay the phone bills and jobs sold through my company. He would pay for the materials and installing any job, whoever sold by, would split the profits 50-50. I thought this was a good deal, for I would have to spend less time at the office. When we got this deal done it was vacation time, so we were off to Puerto Rico for seven days. Terrists blowed up, I think, nine military planes. We heard the explosions from our room because it was close to the air field. The next day we took a plane hop over to St. Thomas. Florence didn't go with us. We made dinner reservations for five o'clock. There were rumors that a bomb was in one of the civilian planes and we had trouble getting a plane back. We had to take any plane available, then we couldn't get passage together. Florence had postponed our reservations three times, and was walking the floor wondering what happened to us. Finally at nine o'clock we made it back, and boy was Florence glad to see us. Next day we took a tour through the jungle and rain forest.

Sunday we come home and got back into our old routine. We were making out our budget. I had the electerial figured out, telephone, the insurance, the trash, and so much for grocerys and misc. Added it all up and showed the amount to Florence and she said that's not right. You don't have the credit card amount. She told me what the amount was, and I said you have gotten carried away with those cards. The interest was from 20-24%. She had been buying things, not because we needed them, but mostly because they were on sale.

I told her she was going to get mad at me for what I'm going to do, but in six months you will kiss me and thank me for paying them off. We will tear up your credit cards and we will not have any more cards. You can buy more by paying cash than using credit cards.

One day she ups and kisses me, and I said what was that for, and she said it was for getting rid of those credit cards. I have been able to buy more and have more money in my billfold.

Honey, you are a genius!

I have been watching shoppers at the check out counters. And I find out that 99.9% of shoppers pay with credit cards. I tried to see things they bought. They would have carts full of merchandise, and some of the most expensive goods. I've seen men come in a hardware store and buy $.50 of goods and pay with a credit card. I've saw people in a restaurant and pay their meal with a credit card. It seems the whole country has gone card crazy, and it is out of control. They don't care what an item costs just so they can buy it on their credit card. A credit is too easy to get. Credit card companies advertising on tv and radio, and sending them out through the mail, hoping you will keep them.

There are so many familys in this country that are in credit over their heads. The people of this country are not going to get out of debt intill they start using common sense and living within their own living standards.

Well, it was time for us to take another trip. I checked with Adrian, and he said he had us booked at the Flamingo Hotel and Casino. Florence's emphysema was getting worse. I had to take her to the hospital in Las Vegas. She was released and we enjoyed our stay in Vegas. We settled down at home. Later on, we took a trip to Aruba. This was a very good trip. Once again we returned home and settled down to home life. The next year we went to Brazil in South America. We went up on Sugarloaf Mountain and visited the rain forest. One thing we missed was there was no casino's in Brazil. We was in Brazil ten days. We took our daughter with us and Adrian and Wanda took their daughter Cindy. Our next trip was to Puerto Vallarta in Mexico.. We took one more trip. It was to the Bohama's Paradise Island. By this time Florence's emphazema was getting worse and she did not feel like going on anymore trips. Her lungs were getting real bad. I told her I wouldn't go anywhere without her. She gave me an argument about that. She said she wanted me to at least to keep on going to Las Vegas with Adrian and Wanda. I finally said I would go to Vegas with them, but nowhere else. I went to Vegas three more times with Adrian and Wanda, and one time we took our sister Marie with us.

Brother Adrian decided to sell his business and retire. I thought personaly it was something he should have done sometime ago, as his assets were well over a million dollars, but I had to give Adrian credit for this. He worked for it. Nobody gave him a single thing. He was just a good manager and buisness man. Being Adrian was retiring, I thought it was about time I was quitting the business also, so I closed out my business and turned the company over to my son Randolph.

Florence's Health Declines

Adrian kept going on trips and invited me to go along but I wouldn't because Florence was not able to go. I keep having to take Florence to the hospital more often as her lungs were getting worse. Our family Dr. LeFevre said he had done all he knew how to do. He turned her over to a lung specialist.

Florence didn't like that very much. Ever so often I would have to take her to the hospital. When she would go in right away they would tell her she needed oxygen. When she was released after a week her oxygen was just above the level and they can't recommend oxygen because Medicare won't pay for it. Well I got tired of that old line and I went and bought her a $4800.00 oxygen machine. She gives me heck for buying it, but it eased my mind that I was doing all that I knew how to in helping her. I worry about her. I can't sleep good anymore from worrying about her. She has always said I was the strong one of the family but it isn't so where and if she's involved. I just got back from Betty and Joe More's. Joe is Florence's brother and Betty the sister-in-law. Betty and Florence are real close. Of course, Betty is one of my favorite. Me and her is the only Briar-hoppers in the more family. We rib each other all the time. Betty is from Berea, Kentucky. I took her down a big head of cabbage today and she sent Florence a jar of grape jelly. Florence didn't feel good enough to go with me.

Our daughter Lori will be over tonite with her two girls, Amy and Kary. Those two girls love their grandparents. Amy has helped me in the garden every year since she has been as big as a tadpole. I guess next year we will have help. Kary is wanting to help with everything. Amy comes over and stays Friday night and me and her goes to the Waffle House on Sat. morning. Guess Lori and the girls will be over as they live real close by. The other grandchildren, Sean, Rachel, Ben, Kris. Tod, Scott, Peanut and some that live in Florida they all live to far away to visit very often.

Florence and Lori used to go shopping once a week, but Florence has not went with her the last few times and that worries me. She is not getting any better.

My Great Hurt

On August 20, 1994 I was installing a monitor on the burglar alarm
that I had built. Florence wasn't feeling good on the davenport for
awhile then she went in the kitchen. I had my step ladder setting up
against the kitchen wall by the living room door. I guess Florence
went into the bathroom. I heard her call my name. Then there was
a crash. I said "What did you knock over" and she didn't answer
me. I looked around the door and she was laying on the bathroom
floor. I didn't panic. I give her artificial respiration. I give her the
up and down massage on her chest. I give her oxygen but she died
in my arms while I was waiting on 911.

That was the day my life stopped. I'll never forget nor will I ever
be the same. Death is so sudden. They die and you get two or three
hours, and from there three to four days, they are buried, and you
will never see them again in this world.

Florence & Me

Conclusion

This is a summary and status of the John Cleveland and Bessie Ginter family.

John Cleveland (Pop) passed away in 1971 at the age of 88. He was in sufficient financial shape that Mom didn't have to worry the rest of her life.

Raymond, the oldest, passed away in 1983 at the age of 74. Raymond owned his home in Middletown Ohio. He raised a family of 5. He was a widower the last 12 years and was living good.

Walter, age 83 retired from GM, owns a home in Michigan and a winter home in Florida, in good financial shape, enough to last him and his wife Vickie the rest of their lived.

I am now a widower. I own a 12 room house and 3 acres of land at Pleasant Hill, Ohio. I have enough income to last me the rest of my life. Age 79.

Austin owns a couple of properties and has made good money the last 30 years. I do not know his financial status. It shoud be good Age 77.

Marie, age 74, has been a widow for the last 25 years, owns her own home, was married to Bud Baker, also owns a rental property, and has sufficient income to last her the rest of her life.

Harold Adrian Ginter, age 70, retired a millionaire, owned and operated a home improvement company.

Virginia is the youngest. Her and her husband Louis Dudas owns their home in Dayton Ohio. Louis is retired from Wright Patterson airfield. He was a civilian employe.

They should have enough money to last them.

Bessie(Mom) passed away in 1985 at age 96. Mom and Pop was proud of the way the children turned out, and would be more proud today, knowing their status. Not one of the children has a high school education. In fact no one in the John Cleveland and Bessie Ginter family had above a 11th grade education. Pop, Mom and all the children had good minds and good common sense thinking and all did well in the generation we lived in.

"There will never be another like it."

THE END

Historical Photographs & Family Images

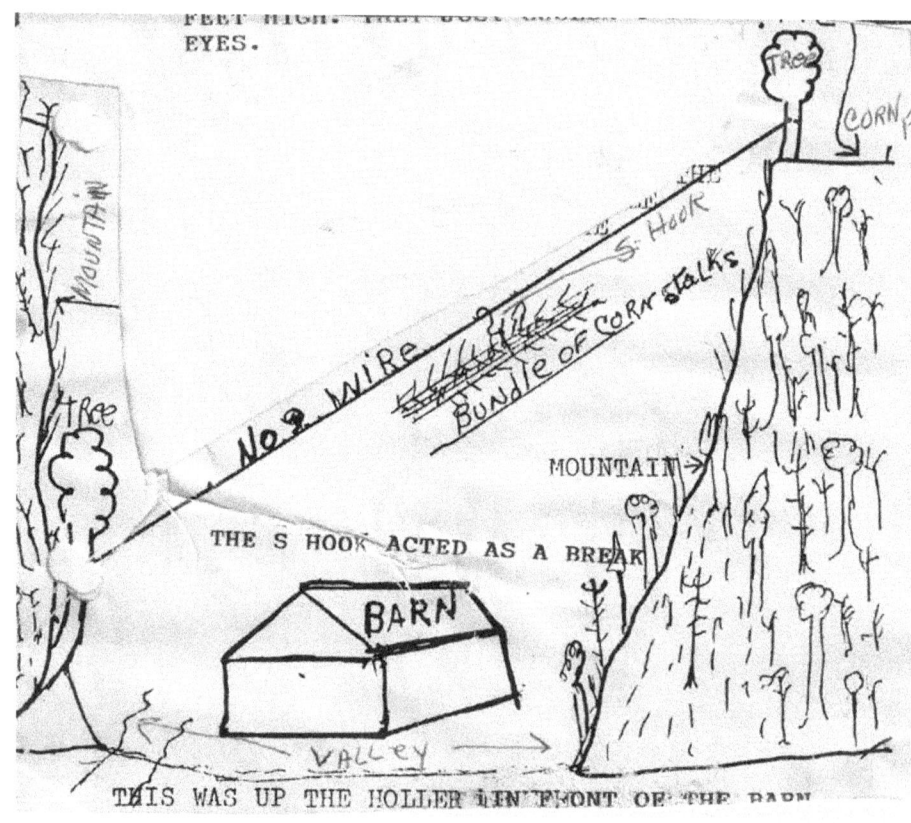

Corn Zipline

Pop and Mom at Sycmore Street

Top: Pop, Walter, Mom Bottom: Austin, Gma Rollins, Adrian

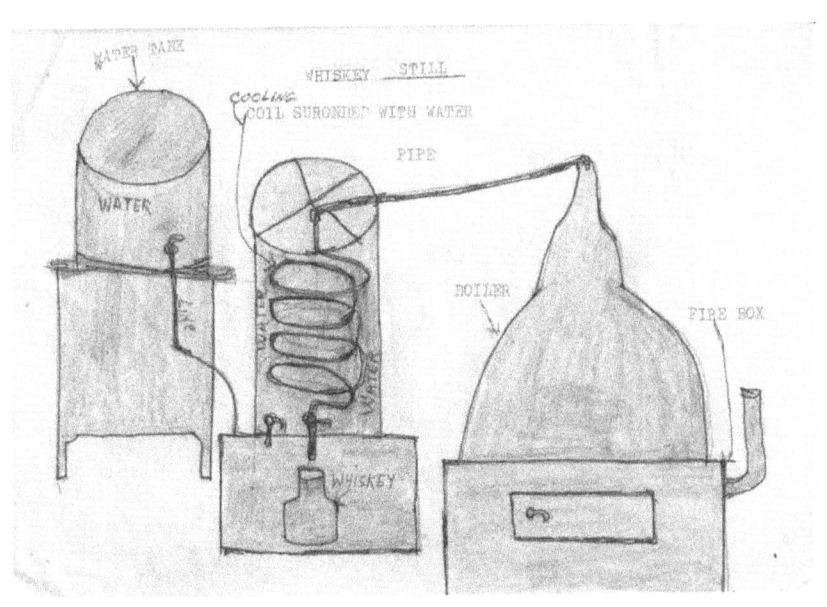

Hand Drawed Moonshine Still

Gma Sarah Prudence (Miller) Rollins (L) &

Gma Nancy Cordelia (Myhnier) Ginter at the Rollins house

Aunt Anna May(Rollins) Stamper

Menifee Man Held
In Fatal Shooting

Refuses to Talk Except to Admit Firing Shot, Jailer Says.

Special to The Courier-Journal.

Frenchburg. Ky.. Nov. 18.—Burton Ingram. 23 years old. is in the Menifee County jail here awaiting arraignment tomorrow on charges of fatally shooting Sid Spencer. 22, on Beaver Creek. near Scranton. yesterday. Beyond admitting that he fired the shot. Ingram has refused to talk about the case, according to Jailer Jasper Williams.

The two youths were said to have left Scranton a short time before the shooting. coming toward Frenchburg. The bullet took effect near Spencer's heart. There are said to be no witnesses.

The victim is a son of Jess Spencer and belongs to a widely-known family in Menifee County. Ingram. a son of Buddie Ingram. is to be arraigned tomorrow morning before County Judge Elmer McGlothin.

Sid Spencer Murder

109

1967 Top: Me, Marie, Raymond, Virginia, Adrian. Seated Pop,
Mom

Front: Adrian, Me. Rear: Pop Raymond

Mom, Me, Pop

1981 Rear: Walter, Marie, Me, Adrian. Front: Raymond, Mom, Virginia

Bobby Osborne Late 1940s

Bobby Osborne, Little Jimmy Dickens ,Larry Richardson

Louise Osborne, Me, Sonny Osborne

Me & Onions

Book Typed on Manual Typewriter

Hand Drawed Wagon

Ginter Cemetary

Ginter Cemetary on top of Leatherwood Branch

James Monroe and Cordelia Ginter-Ginter Cemetary

Wade & Sarah Rollins-Ginter Cemetery

Menifee County Historical Marker

Murder Branch Massacre

Mom and Pop Ginter - 1950s

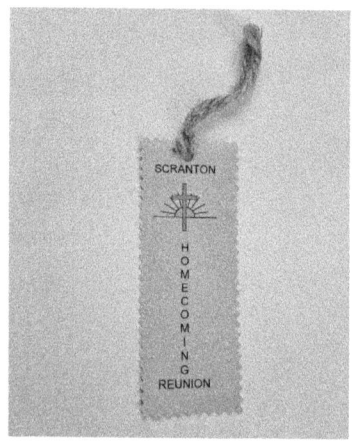

Scranton Homecoming 2000

Scranton Homecoming 2001

About the Author

Otto Fleenor Ginter was born September 3, 1915 in Menifee County, Kentucky to John Cleveland Ginter and Bessie (Rollins) Ginter. He was from a family of seven children. Dad was a self taught man, only reaching the 7th grade in school. His early life was full of adventure and learning how to survive during the depression. These were lessons that he used throughout his life. He was an honest man who thought that a man's word and a handshake was as good as a contract. Dad was a hard worker and held many overlapping jobs.

Dad loved Mom and mourned her greatly. He took care of Mom, her mom and dad, two step-sons, one adopted daughter, sister Lori and me. He returned many times to his beloved Menifee to visit and reminisce the old days. The last thing he ever did was go visit Menifee on Easter weekend 1996. He died eight days later. He is with Mom…

-Randolph Eugene Ginter

Otto Fleenor Ginter (1915-1996)